BEYOND THE SHADE
of the
MANGO TREE

BEYOND THE SHADE

of the

MANGO TREE

Reflections on What God Sees in Us

EDWARD DUBE

Foreword by Tad R. Callister

DESERET
BOOK

Library of Congress Cataloging-in-Publication Data

Names: Dube, Edward, 1962– author. | Callister, Tad R., 1945– writer of foreword.

Title: Beyond the shade of the mango tree : reflections on what God sees in us / Edward Dube ; foreword by Tad R. Callister.

Description: Salt Lake City : Deseret Book, [2021] | Includes bibliographical references. | Summary: "An exploration of faith in God by Elder Edward Dube of The Church of Jesus Christ of Latter-day Saints"—Provided by publisher.

Identifiers: LCCN 2021007169 | ISBN 9781629729190 (hardback)

Subjects: LCSH: Christian life—Mormon authors. | Spiritual life—The Church of Jesus Christ of Latter-day Saints.

Classification: LCC BX8656 .D78 2021 | DDC 248.4/893—dc23

LC record available at https://lccn.loc.gov/2021007169

Printed in the United States of America

Lake Book Manufacturing, Inc., Melrose Park, IL

10   9   8   7   6   5   4   3   2   1

Contents

Contents

FOREWORD

by Tad R. Callister

Regardless of the poverty we may suffer, the despair we may feel, the guilt we may carry, or the failures we may experience, there is one doctrine more than any other that can give us hope. It is the doctrine of godhood—the assurance that through Jesus Christ and His Atonement, we can not only return to God's presence but also become like Him.

This book is a vivid reminder that each of us is a child of God with the divine potential to become like Him, whether we were born in a rural village in Africa—as was Elder Edward Dube, who plowed his fields with a donkey—or in an urban center of the United States, with the latest technology at our command. This book is a living testimony that external qualities such as race, wealth, and status do not control our eternal destiny. Rather, our destiny is determined by internal decisions, usually made one small choice at a time.

The scriptures teach that "with God all things are possible" (Matthew 19:26). If we choose to accept this statement at face value, we begin to see new vistas of possibilities never before dreamed of. This truth converts our thinking from focusing on mortal limitations to focusing on divine possibilities. It helps us realize that the Savior's crowning aim is not just to cleanse us but to perfect us. We discover that God sees us not as mere mortals but as potential gods and goddesses.

Elder Dube teaches this truth powerfully, from the scriptures and with personal and intimate stories from his own life. As we read about his experiences, we see that it was as though one curtain after another was lifted until he finally began to see his godly potential. And with that increased vision of who he might become, he has found increased motivation to become that very person.

He tells the story of a step-by-step ascent—from resisting the restored gospel to fully embracing it as a 22-year-old convert, the only member of The Church of Jesus Christ of Latter-day Saints in his family at the time; from being afraid of sharing his testimony to doing so with power and authority from God; from suffering with an inferiority complex to serving with compelling confidence that God is with him on this mortal journey.

He tells of his postmission courtship with the first convert he taught and of his leap of faith to get married in spite of having only minimal financial resources; of his 15-kilometer (9.3-mile) walk to church each week; of withstanding family pressure to put cultural traditions ahead of gospel principles; and of overcoming his own racial prejudice so he could learn to love all men and women as God does.

Each experience has been a refining influence in his life, polishing his rough edges and enhancing his vision of who the Lord wants him to become. This vision has unfolded before him: that there are no mortal restrictions or weaknesses that God cannot help him conquer. Through his experiences, he has begun to see himself as God sees him.

In a real sense, Elder Dube's story is the story of many of God's children—at first a story of doubt and struggle and hardship and resignation of one's lot in life, later a story of enhanced enlightenment and hope, and finally a realization that he can become all that God wants him to be.

And this is the theme of this book: God has endowed us, as His offspring, with the divine composition to become like Him. His Beloved Son, Jesus Christ, has carried out the Atonement to unleash that potential and plant in our minds and hearts the vision of its reality. As you read this book, you will begin to see yourself as God sees you and feel inspired and encouraged to work toward that exalted end.

Acknowledgments

As I share this book, I owe a debt of gratitude to my mother, Rose Moyo Dube (1934–1997), who continues to inspire me from the other side of the veil. Her simple, loving teachings have, to a large extent, motivated me to write this book. I also express my love and appreciation to my best friend—my wife, Naume—for her patience and constant encouragement. I am thankful to our children—Rosemary, Rachel, Edward Jr., and Edith—who have all graduated or will soon graduate from Brigham Young University, fulfilling their parents' dreams, and to our son-in-law, Riley Reeves, for his boundless encouragement to work on this project. I am, of course, indebted to my father, Clement Matarirano Nzuwa Dube (1932–1993), who taught me principles of integrity that resonate with me to this day.

I am also profoundly grateful for the many men and women with whom I have served in the Church. In one way or another, they have all contributed to the development of this book.

Lisa Roper, my product director at Deseret Book, has been immensely helpful and patient with me, providing constructive feedback on how to improve the manuscript. Jerry James also read a draft of the manuscript and offered insightful recommendations for improvement.

In the production of this manuscript, I was assisted by Aaron Louis West. Aaron's insights about the composition of readable text and his extensive doctrinal background helped me refine the manuscript. He has been more than an editor. And he has from time to time consulted with his dear wife, Emma, who in turn has shared valuable ideas for improvement. Sister Renetta Felt West's profound insights made a great contribution to the manuscript. Our friends Jeffrey Reuel and Ramona Daw Pomeroy proofread the manuscript and made recommendations, for which I am profoundly grateful.

Elder Tad R. Callister, a mentor and brother whose writing and teaching I have observed from a distance over the years, read the finished product and gave very helpful recommendations, including a suggestion to add a chapter to the book. I am deeply grateful for his counsel. He not only provided constructive insights but agreed to write the foreword.

Notwithstanding the excellent contributions and suggestions of these many great people, I am solely responsible for what is written in this book.

I sincerely express my appreciation to all those who have crossed my path in this mortal journey of striving to see ourselves as God sees us and ultimately become like Him.

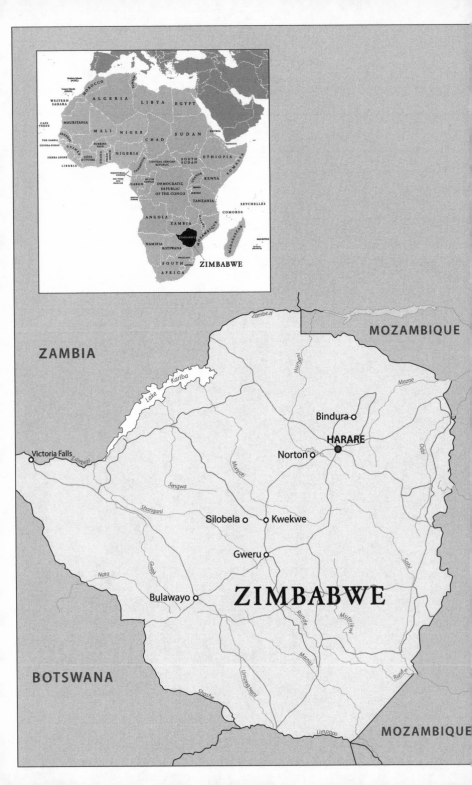

Leaving the Comfort
of the Shade

I love the account of Alma teaching his son Helaman to take care of the Nephites' sacred records. Whenever I read it, I visualize Alma and Helaman sitting in the shade of a mango tree.

Why a mango tree? Because of experiences I had in Silobela, the rural village where I was born and raised. When I was born, Silobela was in the nation of Southern Rhodesia, a British colony. Three years later, the name of the nation was changed to Rhodesia. In 1980, we gained independence and called our nation Zimbabwe.

For the first 15 years of my life, my family's home—*musha* in my native language of Shona—was a group of small, round huts made of logs covered with mud. The huts had thatch for roofs and dried cow dung for floors. The central hut was a kitchen and a family-gathering area. The adjacent huts were bedrooms—one for our parents, one for the boys, and one for our only sister.

Mango trees close to our home provided fruit and shade. In that shade, my mother sometimes taught my siblings and me, just as I picture Alma teaching Helaman.

Edward's childhood home, in Silobela, Zimbabwe, with mango trees nearby. This photograph was taken in 2020. The walls of the huts are now reinforced with brick, not the sticks that formed the walls when Edward lived there. The roofs are much the same now as they were then.

Lessons Learned beyond the Shade

Of course, we can't learn everything we need to know if we stay in the comfort of a tree's shade. Helaman and I both learned this truth from our parents.

Alma instructed his son to keep a record of the people and to take care of the plates of brass and the 24 gold plates of the Jaredites (see Alma 37:1–5, 21). Today we are blessed to have a portion of those records compiled in the Book of Mormon.

I am fascinated by Alma's counsel to Helaman. He said that it might seem foolish to work so hard to preserve these words. But he observed, "By small and simple things are great things brought to pass" (Alma 37:6). He testified that those words had brought many to "rejoice in Jesus Christ their Redeemer" and that they could bring the same blessing to "many thousands" more (Alma 37:9–10).

Alma taught Helaman to do more than keep a record and protect sacred plates. He instructed his son to preach repentance and faith in Jesus Christ (see Alma 37:33). He said: "Learn wisdom in thy youth; yea, learn in thy youth to keep the commandments of God. Yea, and cry unto God for all thy support; yea, let all thy doings be unto the Lord, and whithersoever thou goest let it be in the Lord" (Alma 37:35–36).

To follow this counsel, Helaman had to leave the comfort of the shade. He and his brothers and other missionaries went forth declaring the word of God and leading the people to "continual peace" and "exceedingly great prosperity" (Alma 49:30). He later moved even farther away from the shade, to the heat of the battlefield. He "march[ed] at the head of his two thousand stripling soldiers" (Alma 53:22)—young men who were determined to protect their families and "to keep the commandments of God and to walk uprightly before him" (Alma 53:21).

In addition to serving as a prophet and military leader, Helaman was a loving and dedicated father. Four years after he died, his son Helaman accepted the responsibility to take care of the plates. The younger Helaman "did walk after the ways of his father" (Helaman 3:20), serving as a great prophet and leader. He shared his testimony and counsel with his own sons Nephi and Lehi as they prepared for their ministry. The power of his words showed that he, like his father, had learned lessons beyond the shade of the mango tree.

"My sons," he said, "remember, remember that it is upon the rock of our Redeemer, who is Christ, the Son of God, that ye must build your foundation; that when the devil shall send forth his mighty winds, yea, his shafts in the whirlwind, yea, when all his hail and his mighty storm shall beat upon you, it shall have no power over you to drag you down to the gulf of misery and endless wo, because of the rock upon which ye are built, which is a sure foundation, a foundation whereon if men build they cannot fall" (Helaman 5:12).

Like Alma's counsel to Helaman, my mother's teaching helped me move beyond the comfort of the shade. In fact, I learned some of Mother's most impactful lessons far away from mango trees. We owned land about five to seven kilometers (three to four miles) away, where we raised crops. My siblings and I worked side by side with Mother in the fields, in the heat of the sun. She took advantage of that time to teach us.

Late one morning, we had been hoeing in the fields for what I felt was a very long time. I stopped to look back at what we had accomplished and said, "Look at all we have done!" Mother did not respond. Thinking that she had not heard me, I repeated what I had said, this time a little louder. Again she did not reply. Raising my voice a little more, I said it once again. Finally, she turned to me and said, "Edward, never look back. Look ahead at what we still have to do!" She pointed to the field in front of us, which was still full of weeds.

My mother was not saying that we shouldn't rejoice in our successes; she was saying that we shouldn't let what we have done keep us from doing what we need to do now. She was not saying that we shouldn't learn from the past; she was saying that we should move forward into the future with determination and faith.

That day in the field, I began learning to see beyond what I thought I knew, beyond what I could have experienced if I had stayed in the shade of the mango tree. When Mother told me to look ahead, she taught me a principle that would one day give me courage to embrace the restored gospel of Jesus Christ. Her lesson continues to inspire me today.

More Than We Think We Know

I believe that each of us has a personal "mango tree"—a place that, for a time, is all we know. It might be a safe and happy place or a troubled and dangerous one. It might be a farm or an apartment complex, a town or a city, a school or a church. It might just be a state of mind. But at some point, each of us needs to be ready for the Lord to show us more: More than we think we know about our environment. More than we think we know about Him. More than we think we know about ourselves.

For me, this journey began as I learned from my parents and other family members. It continued as I learned from Catholic priests, including one priest who taught me in the shade of another mango tree. It accelerated as I learned from the Book of Mormon and from friends and missionaries in The Church of Jesus Christ of Latter-day Saints. I persist in that journey today, striving to follow the whisperings of the Holy Spirit and the counsel of living prophets.

I treasure the experiences and lessons of my childhood, and I have found joy in learning more. I still have much to learn. We all have much to learn. More than that, we have much to *do*—because as we allow the Lord to teach us more about Himself and more about ourselves, He prepares us to participate in His work. As Alma taught Helaman, we help the Lord "bring about his great and eternal purposes" not by taking great strides but by doing "small and simple things" (Alma 37:6–7)—saying personal and family prayers, studying the scriptures daily, holding family home evening, loving one another, being sincere and honest, treating family members and others with kindness and gentleness.

This book draws from teachings of latter-day prophets and apostles, ancient and modern scriptures, and my personal experiences. It is about Jesus Christ—about His power to change us into the men and women He knows we can become. As you read, I invite you to join me on this journey to learn of Him, walk in His covenant path, and submit joyfully to His will. My hope is that I might say something that will serve as a catalyst to help you strengthen your faith and tap your full potential as a child of God.

My prayer is that we will all open our eyes to the Lord's goodness, love, and power. Beyond opening our eyes, I hope we will open our hearts and draw near to our Savior and Redeemer. As we do, He will expand our vision. He will teach us to see beyond the shade of the mango tree—to see what He and our Heavenly Father see in us.

Shall we not go on in so great a cause?
Go forward and not backward.
Courage, . . . and on, on to the victory!
Let your hearts rejoice, and be exceedingly glad.

DOCTRINE AND COVENANTS 128:22

PART I

OPENING OUR EYES

We know in part. . . .

For now we see through a glass, darkly;

but then face to face.

1 CORINTHIANS 13:9, 12

CHAPTER 1

A Mother's Trust in God

President David O. McKay taught this profound lesson about the influence of a mother: "Motherhood is the greatest potential influence either for good or ill in human life. The mother's image is the first that stamps itself on the unwritten page of the young child's mind."[1]

Helaman's 2,000 young warriors felt that influence. They were willing to fight for the liberty of their families because "they had been taught by their mothers, that if they did not doubt, God would deliver them." They told their leader, "We do not doubt our mothers knew it" (Alma 56:47–48).

In my childhood, I learned to trust God as I listened to my mother pray. She prayed as though God was standing right there in our little hut. At times, I opened my eyes, just to see if He was there. Mother always prayed for each child in the family, mentioning specific challenges we faced and pleading with God to protect us from the evils of the world. Whenever I felt tempted to do something wrong, I would hear my mother's voice in my mind, pleading with God for my protection. Her voice came with such freshness and impact that I felt as though she was with me.

I also learned to trust God as I witnessed my mother's actions *after* she prayed. One experience stands out.

A Stolen Donkey

My parents were farmers, so I worked in the fields from the time I was a little boy. My father taught me to start each day at 4:00 a.m., the time he saw a certain star in a certain position in the sky. To this day I do not need an alarm clock to wake up at that hour.

I helped plow, plant, weed, and harvest the crops. I also fetched water from a borehole about 7.5 kilometers (4.7 miles) from my home. I walked the whole way, either pushing a 200-liter (53-gallon) drum or using donkeys to pull a cart.

The only resources we had for cultivating the fields were four donkeys and a plow. One summer while we were in the middle of preparing the fields for planting, we realized that one of our donkeys was missing. We quickly discovered that it had been stolen by a well-known, cunning thief in the village.

My siblings and I were devastated and heartbroken. Now we would have to plow with a team of two donkeys instead of four. This development would slow us down and cause many more hours of work. And our father wasn't there to help us. He was working far away from home and would not return for another 8 to 12 weeks.

A Mother's Prayer

At the end of that day, Mother gathered us and asked us to kneel in prayer, as we did each night before we went to bed. I kneeled with my sister, Theresa, and my brothers Cosmos,

Clement, and Obert. Onismo, our baby brother, lay quietly on the floor with a blanket wrapped around him. We heard our mother plead with God that our donkey be returned to us. After praying, she asked us to go to bed. Obediently, we went to the adjacent huts—one for the boys, one for Theresa—where we fell asleep on the floor, cushioned by dried cow dung.

Acting with Trust in God

Early the next morning before I left for school, I was preparing two of our remaining three donkeys to plow the fields. Mother came to me with a smile on her face and a firmness in her voice. "Edward," she said, "do not worry. We will get our donkey back!"

I hesitantly responded, "Good." I was taught not to question my elders, especially my parents, but I doubted. I wondered how we could possibly get our donkey back. Everyone in the village knew that once this man claimed your donkey, goat, or cow, that was the end of it.

Mother filed a donkey theft report with the local authorities. She was invited to appear in court or have her representative appear, but we were too poor to afford a lawyer, so she and I went alone. In contrast, the thief was powerful and well-connected, and he had a lawyer. He was often challenged in court, but he never lost a case.

When the judge asked Mother why she claimed that this was her donkey, she simply said that it was her donkey. She then asked that the accused thief identify all the donkey's features, including any visible marks on the animal.

The thief's lawyer insisted that Mother describe the donkey, but she declined. She told the jury that my father had put a special mark on the donkey and that he had placed the same mark on three other donkeys, which were outside the courtroom. I was outside with the animals, waiting to show them to the judge and the jury.

The accused thief finally agreed to describe the features of the donkey. When he finished, Mother asked, "What about a circle mark? Tell the court—are you aware of it?"

In response to this question, the man made a blunder. He asked Mother where the mark was. Mother chuckled and said that since he claimed the donkey was his, he should tell the court himself. When the man and his lawyer couldn't respond, the judge asked Mother to go outside, where she claimed the other three donkeys were, and show him the circle marks on them and on the stolen donkey. Sure enough, on the left front leg, father had used a hot round steel to mark all his donkeys. The judge ordered the thief to return the donkey and pay damages.

When Mother and I came home with four donkeys that evening, my siblings and I began to celebrate, jumping up and down with excitement. But we heard our mother's voice above ours. "Wait, wait, wait," she said. "We need to thank God for this." She asked us to kneel and thank God for giving her ideas and courage. She knew all along He would help us get our donkey back.

After this experience, I no longer opened my eyes when Mother prayed, trying to see if God was there. I knew He *was* there. I couldn't see Him, but I didn't have to. My mother had helped me open my eyes to His great power and infinite compassion, even for our little family. I was starting to learn that "God is our refuge and strength, a very present help in trouble" (Psalm 46:1). He loves us, and He is always ready to answer our prayers—through the whisperings of the Spirit, through the

Four donkeys plowing a field in Silobela, Zimbabwe, 2015

service we give one another, through miracles great and small. Every individual and every family can trust Him, just as my mother and our family did.

> Trust in the Lord with all thine heart;
> and lean not unto thine own understanding.
>
> In all thy ways acknowledge him,
> and he shall direct thy paths.
>
> PROVERBS 3:5–6

CHAPTER 2

Early Impressions from the Spirit

"Learn of me," the Savior says, "and listen to my words; walk in the meekness of my Spirit, and you shall have peace in me" (Doctrine and Covenants 19:23). Each disciple of Jesus Christ takes a journey to accept this invitation and follow this command.

This journey is a continual process that requires us to keep moving forward, regardless of our weaknesses, limitations, and trials. The Lord helps us understand that although the journey will not be easy, He will bless and strengthen us along the way. He revealed to the Prophet Joseph Smith: "I give unto you a commandment, that ye shall forsake all evil and cleave unto all good, that ye shall live by every word which proceedeth forth out of the mouth of God. For he will give unto the faithful line upon line, precept upon precept; and I will try you and prove you herewith. And whoso layeth down his [or her] life in my cause, for my name's sake, shall find it again, even life eternal" (Doctrine and Covenants 98:11–13).

This is our course: learning of the Savior line upon line and progressing toward eternal life. If we are willing to follow this course, the Lord blesses us with guides to help us. One of my early guides was the Roman Catholic Church. My experiences in the Catholic Church helped me open my eyes to the Savior's love and power, contributing to the foundation I needed to live as His disciple.

Learning through Symbolism and Recitation

When I was 10 years old, I traveled to the Loreto Roman Catholic Mission, about 32 kilometers (20 miles) from my rural home in Silobela. I spent two weeks there, learning about confirmation, one of the seven sacraments of the Catholic Church. When faithful Catholics receive confirmation, they believe they are sealed with the gift of the Holy Spirit. They receive strength in their determination to live a Christian life.

As I learned about confirmation, I prepared to receive a rosary—a necklace that guides a special Catholic prayer. I learned about the symbolism of each bead on a rosary. To begin the rosary prayer, an individual holds the crucifix on the necklace and recites the Apostles' Creed—a statement of belief in the Father, the Son, and the Holy Spirit. Then the person follows the beads on the necklace, reciting other texts, such as the Lord's Prayer (see Matthew 6:9–13) and Mary's words of testimony to her cousin Elizabeth (see Luke 1:46–55). This pattern of recitation and prayer contributed significantly to my development of faith in Heavenly Father and Jesus Christ.

After I received the confirmation, the Catholic priest placed a rosary around my neck. He looked into my eyes and said, "You are the light of the world." Then, pointing to a burning candle, he quoted the Savior's words: "Let your light so shine before men, that they may see your good works, and glorify your Father which is in heaven" (Matthew 5:16). Those words entered my mind and heart and inspired me to follow the example of Jesus Christ.

Learning to Repent

As a confirmed member of the Catholic Church, I had the privilege to partake of communion—a small piece of bread and a sip of wine in remembrance of Jesus Christ's suffering. A priest visited our little congregation once a month and administered the communion. I always looked forward to that occasion.

Whenever the priest visited us, we had the opportunity to meet with him to confess our sins to the Lord. I recall walking under a mango tree, where the priest sat on a chair. I kneeled in front of him and confessed my sins—things like treating my siblings unkindly, lying to the school authorities when I was late for school to avoid punishment, stealing my mother's peanut butter from a jar, and having improper thoughts.

I enjoyed the feeling I received after confessing. I was happy, and I wanted the feeling to stay. I felt clean. I did not want to disappoint the Lord. I did not want the priest to think I was not serious about changing and being clean. I even remember asking my siblings not to tempt me so that I would remain clean before my Lord.

From the priest under the mango tree, I learned that repentance is not a casual act. One day I went to him and confessed—as I had already confessed over and over again—that I had stolen peanut butter from my mother's jar. He was not pleased. He said, "Edward, do not play with God. Repentance means turning away from sin." This was not easy for me, but eventually, with my mother's help, I was able to stop stealing peanut butter.

Learning about the Life and Mission of Jesus Christ

Each time I went to our Catholic chapel, I gazed at the walls, which displayed scenes from the Savior's life. Studying those pictures, I learned of Jesus Christ's birth, and I learned of Him teaching in the temple, praying in the Garden of Gethsemane, carrying the cross to Calvary, and being crucified at Golgotha.

Each time I looked at the depiction of the Crucifixion, with those nails in the Savior's hands and feet and those thorns on His head, I was saddened. My eyes filled with tears, and I said to myself, "Hey! He really went through a lot . . . just for me!"

Preparing to Receive the Fullness of the Gospel

At a tender age, I learned of the Lord and began to look to Him with worship and gratitude. Certain elements of Catholicism—recitation, symbolism, words from kind priests, and pictures of the Savior's life and mission—combined to instill in me desires to do good and to be of service to others. Later in my life, I learned that these desires were impressions from the Holy Spirit, preparing me to receive the fullness of the gospel of Jesus Christ and become the man God wanted me to become.

My Catholic confirmation at the age of 10 prepared me to receive the gift of the Holy Ghost years later so I could have that member of the Godhead as my "constant companion" (Doctrine and Covenants 121:46).

The rosary prayer taught me to love my Heavenly Father and exercise faith in Him. This faith has now increased, leading me to "pray always, and not faint" (2 Nephi 32:9)—to approach Him "with real intent" (Moroni 7:6).

Years after a Catholic priest counseled me to "let [my] light so shine before men," I accepted a call to serve as a missionary and share the restored gospel of Jesus Christ.

My monthly experiences with the communion prepared me to receive the sacrament weekly, witnessing to Heavenly Father that I am "willing to take upon [myself] the name of [his] Son, and always remember him and keep his commandments which he has given [me]; that [I] may always have his Spirit to be with [me]" (Doctrine and Covenants 20:77).

In the shade of the mango tree, the Catholic priest taught me to take repentance seriously and to respect the justice of God. Later, as I studied the Book of Mormon, I moved beyond the shade of that tree and learned more about divine mercy: "As often as my people repent will I forgive them their trespasses against me" (Mosiah 26:30). I learned that as long as our repentance is sincere, the Savior will heal us even of our bad habits.

I am grateful for the pictures on the wall in our Catholic chapel. My understanding is deeper now than it was when I gazed at those pictures as a little boy. Through the Book of Mormon, the teachings of latter-day prophets, and continuing impressions from the Holy Spirit, I have built on that early foundation. More and more each day, I am grateful that my Father sent His Beloved Son to carry out the infinite Atonement. Those words I thought as a little boy—"Hey! He really went through a lot . . . just for me!"—are still true. Now, as I strive to follow the Living Christ, I continue to marvel at all He sees in me and all He has done, just for me. I am grateful for all He has done for each member of my family and for each one of my brothers and sisters throughout the world.

> Eye hath not seen, nor ear heard, neither have
> entered into the heart of man, the things which
> God hath prepared for them that love him.
>
> 1 CORINTHIANS 2:9

CHAPTER 3

The Ministry of Angels in Our Families

When we think of angels, we usually think of heavenly beings who deliver messages from God to His children on the earth. I believe in these angels—Michael, Gabriel, Moroni, and others. I also think of some people around us "as though they were angels sent from God to save [us] from everlasting destruction" (Alma 27:4). Often those ministering angels are members of our own family or our extended family.

In my youth, my mother, my father, and an uncle were ministering angels to me. At a trying time in my life, their influence helped me look up to the Lord.

Caught Up in Political Turmoil

At age 15, my siblings and I lived with my mother in Silobela while my father worked in the city of Harare, about 275 kilometers (170 miles) away. The year was 1977—a time of intense political turmoil. Our nation, a British colony at the time, was in the middle of a civil war, with local African groups revolting against the white-minority government. Leaders of that government had declared a state of emergency in Silobela and had imposed martial law. Everyone had to stay indoors after 5:00 p.m. every day.

The year before, I had graduated from primary school. The only way for me to continue my education was to go away to boarding school, but my parents didn't have enough money for that. Without school to keep me occupied, I became interested in the conflict all around me. It seemed to me that all the people in Silobela—men, women, youth, and children—were involved in politics, even though it was dangerous. Caught up in this excitement, I joined one of the major political parties fighting for liberation, and I was elected district secretary in the party's youth group.

Sometimes I traveled from our rural area to attend political rallies in surrounding cities. Those rallies were exciting and infectious. The leaders' speeches fascinated me and stirred my emotions, and I decided to fight for liberation rather than prepare for more education. My friends and I even talked about joining the party's military group in nearby Zambia.

My Angel Mother

I didn't tell my mother about my military plans, but she sensed that something was going on. She always looked up to the Lord, and He blessed her with impressions about how to help her children. Acting on those feelings, she sent me to the city of Gweru to deliver a letter to my father's brother—my Uncle Rafaeri. Obediently, I set out on the long trip to Gweru, about 80 kilometers (50 miles) away. I left the mysterious letter folded in my bag, knowing that it was addressed to my uncle, not to me. I figured that if my mother had wanted me to know its contents, she would have shared it with me.

When I arrived in Gweru, I gave the letter to Uncle Rafaeri.

He explained that he couldn't read, and he handed the letter back to me and asked me to read it to him. As I read, I was surprised to see that the letter was about me! Mother had a message for me, and she knew I would receive it if I read it aloud to my uncle. She wrote that she was concerned about my involvement in politics. She said that the liberation leaders

Rose, Edward's mother (center left), with her sister Sophia Munyavi and two of Sophia's grandchildren, 1985

encouraged rural youth to join the revolution but sent their own children to school. After hearing my mother's letter, Uncle Rafaeri invited me to stay with him in Gweru, and he urged me to get out of politics. I was reluctant at first, but my uncle went out of his way to be good to me. Eventually I accepted his invitation.

My Angel Uncle

During my time in Gweru, Uncle Rafaeri had a profound impact on my life. He always called me *Baba*, which means "father" in my native language of Shona, because I was named after his father—my grandfather. He also called me by that name because I was the eldest of my siblings and the eldest grandchild on my father's side of the family. He helped me see my role as a family leader. Whenever I did something unwise, he said, "No! That is bad! You are the father! You have to set the right example!" In this way and countless others, Uncle Rafaeri helped shape my character.

Uncle Rafaeri knew that the best way to raise children is to help them see their potential. He understood Solomon's proverb:

"Train up a child in the way he should go: and when he is old, he will not depart from it" (Proverbs 22:6). Years later, when my wife and I welcomed children into our family, we tried to follow my uncle's example. We observed that our children wanted to do good when we treated them according to their true identity and potential as children of God. They developed high expectations for themselves and followed their righteous desires to stay on the covenant path. Reprimands would not have inspired them in that way.

My Angel Father

In 1978, I moved to the city of Kwekwe. I stayed with my mother's sister Lorcadia for a while and then moved out on my own. I hoped to find a job and continue my education. When I applied for work at a steel company, an employee in the personnel department told me that if I wanted to be hired, I would have to change the surname on my identification card to match the surname of a man who worked at the plant.

Although my father worked far away, he continued to watch over us. When he heard about the unusual requirement at the steel company, he counseled me not to compromise my integrity. I followed his counsel and withdrew my application at the steel company. I soon found another job and enrolled in school. From this experience, I learned to be unwaveringly honest, moral, and ethical, even in the midst of corruption.

Reflecting on Miracles in My Life

"From the beginning down through the dispensations," said Elder Jeffrey R. Holland, "God has used angels as His emissaries in conveying love and concern for His children. . . . When we speak of those who are instruments in the hand of God, we are reminded that not all angels are from the other side of the veil. Some of them we walk with and talk with—here, now, every day."[2]

Looking back on my life, I can see that ministering angels in my family have rescued me multiple times.

In 1979, political pressure forced my mother and five siblings to move from Silobela to Kwekwe. We found two rooms for rent and lived there together, with my father still working in Harare. Those were difficult days—the most challenging in my life. We could not go back to our rural home, and my mother had to leave our animals and many other possessions behind. We became refugees in our own country, living in a tiny two-room apartment far away from our home. My siblings were unable to go to school for a while because we could not afford education. To supplement our father's meager income, I found a job and my mother and sister sold vegetables in the market. Even then, we could afford only to pay rent and eat one meal a day—two if we were lucky. But we were safe, and we were together.

As I reflect on my life in the late 1970s, I consider it miraculous that I was protected and preserved. The Lord had a vision of my potential, and He shared that vision with people who loved me. Without their influence, I might have gone to Zambia and become a guerilla fighter. I might have died in the war. I might have been imprisoned for insurrection. I might have abandoned hope for an education and honest employment.

My parents encouraged me to work hard, to exercise unwavering faith in God, to get an education, and to maintain my integrity. I praise God for their wise counsel and support. Uncle Rafaeri encouraged me to be a leader and a father figure to my siblings, cousins, and nephews. I am grateful for his confidence in me.

These angels never gave up on me, even at times when my decisions and actions worried them and caused them pain. They serve as a model for me today when I counsel with parents who grieve because of the poor choices of their children. Because of the influence of my mother, my father, and my uncle—because they never gave up on me—I have come to know that "all things work together for good to them that love God, to them who are the called according to his purpose" (Romans 8:28). I am grateful for the Lord's guidance in my youth through ministering angels in my family.

This can be true for all of us. Mothers, fathers, brothers, sisters, grandparents, aunts, uncles, and cousins can be ministering angels for younger members of the family. And children, grandchildren, nieces, nephews, and little brothers and sisters can serve as instruments in the Lord's hands to help the older ones. As the First Presidency has taught us, "The home is the basis of a righteous life, and no other instrumentality can take its place or fulfill its essential functions in carrying forward this God-given responsibility."[3] In our families, we can support one another in our efforts to draw nearer to the Lord and see ourselves as He sees us.

Parents have a sacred duty to rear their children in love
and righteousness, to provide for their physical and
spiritual needs, and to teach them to love and serve
one another, observe the commandments of God,
and be law-abiding citizens wherever they live.

"THE FAMILY: A PROCLAMATION TO THE WORLD"

CHAPTER 4

Choosing Faith

One day in about 124 BC, families gathered around the temple in the city of Zarahemla. Each family, "from the eldest down to the youngest," pitched their tent "with the door thereof towards the temple" (Mosiah 2:5–6). There they listened to Benjamin, their aged prophet-king, as he delivered what was surely one of the greatest sermons in the history of the world.

The people who understood King Benjamin's sermon became unified in their faith in Jesus Christ. They "all cried with one voice, saying: Yea, we believe all the words which thou hast spoken unto us; and also, we know of their surety and truth, because of the Spirit of the Lord Omnipotent, which has wrought a mighty change in us, or in our hearts, that we have no more disposition to do evil, but to do good continually." They declared, "We are willing to enter into a covenant with our God to do his will, and to be obedient to his commandments in all things that he shall command us, all the remainder of our days" (Mosiah 5:2, 5).

Sadly, "many of the rising generation" later hardened their hearts and separated themselves from their parents' faith. They had not been old enough to understand the words of King Benjamin when he spoke to the people, and "they did not believe the tradition of their fathers" (Mosiah 26:1; see also verses 2–3).

I had a similar experience when I was part of the "rising generation." Through this experience, I learned that even though my parents had set a good example for me, the decision to follow the Savior had to be my own. As President Henry B. Eyring has said, "Faith is not an inheritance; it is a choice."[4]

Wavering Commitment

My commitment to my parents' religion began to waver when I was 12 years old. My parents were Catholics, and they had always insisted that my siblings and I attend a Catholic school, which was a long distance from our home. One year we convinced Mother and Father to allow us to attend Kanye Seventh-day Adventist Primary School, which was only about a mile away from home.

I started sixth grade that year. Because the school was so close, I could go home for lunch and still get back on time for lessons or work. This was not the only thing that was different from my previous school. While the teachers were not supposed to insert Seventh-day Adventist teachings in our lessons, they occasionally did. In addition, a friend from a strong Seventh-day Adventist family often quoted Bible verses that seemed to conflict with things I had learned in the Catholic Church. I began feeling uncomfortable with my parents' faith.

When I shared my feelings with my mother, she became very upset and reminded me that our family was Roman Catholic. I relented and continued attending the Roman Catholic Church with the family. Although I had lost interest in Catholicism, I did not want to upset my parents.

Abandoning Righteous Traditions

A few years later, I lived alone in the city as a 16-year-old. By that time, I had stopped going to church. I had lived for a time with my Uncle Rafaeri and then with my Aunt Lorcadia, both good people but not churchgoers. Without my parents nearby, I didn't have anyone to encourage me to participate in Catholic services. In fact, for several years, I did not attend any church. Looking back, I regret that decision to separate myself from religion. Without religion in my life, without the righteous traditions of my mother and father, I became too laid-back.

I set aside the traditions of waking up early. I no longer had to follow a precise schedule of working in the fields, returning home, and helping with firewood. And so I abandoned the discipline of working hard each day to achieve a certain objective.

I was working and taking correspondence classes, but I was not serious about anything. A shadow hovered over me. I had little desire or motivation to achieve. I was failing to do what my parents had always taught me to do: set challenging goals in my studies and work to achieve them.

I had a job and made a meager living, but I didn't think about the future, as my mother had taught me. She always sifted good ground nuts and maize and set them aside so she could plant them in the next rain season. She never used the seeds, even in dire situations, until it was time to plant them. She preferred the family to go without food rather than eat the seeds. Because of this, we had crops each year, and we never depended on government handouts. Despite my mother's example, I didn't save any of the money I earned.

If I had remained an active participant in my parents' religion, even though I did not agree with all its teachings, I believe I would have worked harder and used my time and money more wisely. Each time I attended a worship service, I would have placed myself in a position to learn something from the Holy Spirit. I certainly would have benefited from the Lord's promise: "For where two or three are gathered together in my name, there am I in the midst of them" (Matthew 18:20). I believe I would have remembered and followed my parents' example. I also believe I would have been proactive in searching for the truth to replace the doubt I felt, and I would have found and embraced the fullness of the restored gospel of Jesus Christ earlier in my life.

Lessons Learned

Why do I share this episode from my life? What can we learn from this experience? I believe we can learn two lessons.

The first lesson is that parents should do all they can to establish a good foundation for their children. Some children will never wander from the righteous traditions of their mother and father. Others, like me, will stray for a time from some traditions. But the teachings and example of their parents will stay in their hearts. When I found the restored gospel of Jesus Christ, many of the truths I learned were reminders of things my parents had taught me by word and deed. They helped me open my eyes so later I could embrace an expanded vision of God's plan for me.

President Russell M. Nelson taught: "Parents are to be living examples of 'kindness, and pure knowledge, which . . . greatly enlarge the soul.' Each mother and father should lay aside selfish interests and avoid any thought of hypocrisy, physical force, or evil speaking. Parents soon learn that each child has an inborn yearning to be free. Each individual wants to make his or her own way. No one wants to be restrained, even by a well-intentioned parent. But all of us can cling to the Lord."[5]

The second lesson is that each of us has a responsibility to choose between unbelief and faith. Many of the rising generation in the days of King Mosiah chose not to believe. "Because of their unbelief they could not understand the word of God; and their hearts were hardened" (Mosiah 26:3).

We should never surrender ourselves to doubt, as I did for a time. Asking questions about our beliefs is fine if it leads us to inquire actively about the truth. But even as we ask questions, we should hold on to what we know and remain true to it. With the passage of time, we will come to understand the things we need to understand. C. S. Lewis wisely asserted: "Whenever you find any statement in Christian writings which you can make nothing of, do not worry. Leave it alone. There will come a day, perhaps years later, when you suddenly see what it meant."[6] And Elder Dieter F. Uchtdorf counseled: "Doubt your doubts before you doubt your faith. We must never allow doubt to hold us prisoner and keep us from the divine love, peace, and gifts that come through faith in the Lord Jesus Christ."[7]

In the end, I experienced the truth of President Eyring's statement that faith is not an inheritance but a choice. I returned to many of the traditions I inherited from my parents. To those traditions, I have added even more: the truth of the restored gospel. Although my mother and father did not join The Church of Jesus Christ of Latter-day Saints in their lifetimes, they did their best to follow the counsel of the writer of Proverbs. They "train[ed] up a child in the way he should go." Now that I am older, I "will not depart from it" (Proverbs 22:6).

This is a choice we can make every day. Because of what we have inherited—and, in some cases, in spite of what we have inherited—we can choose faith.

Cheer up your hearts, and remember that ye are
free to act for yourselves—to choose the way of
everlasting death or the way of eternal life.

2 NEPHI 10:23

CHAPTER 5

The Power of the Word of God

At a time when the Nephites were in physical and spiritual danger, Alma went among them to preach the gospel. He was accompanied by Amulek, Zeezrom, three of Mosiah's sons, and two of his own sons. Alma and his companions shared the gospel because "the preaching of the word had a great tendency to lead the people to do that which was just—yea, it had had more powerful effect upon the minds of the people than the sword, or anything else, which had happened unto them" (Alma 31:5).

In early 1983, at a pivotal time in my life, I began to truly partake of the "powerful effect" of the Lord's word. I was 21 years old at the time. Looking back, I wonder why I waited so long.

My Introduction to the Book of Mormon

Two years earlier, I ignored an opportunity to partake of the word of the Lord. I was working for a man named Leister Heath. As part of my job, I occasionally watched over the Heaths' two boys: Leister Jr., age nine, and Bruce, age seven.

One day while the boys and I were playing games in the yard,

Leister Jr. said to me, "Eddie, do you know that my father is a branch president in our Church?"

I asked, "What is a branch president?"

Leister Jr. explained that his father was the leader of their congregation in The Church of Jesus Christ of Latter-day Saints. I then told this nine-year-old boy that his father was wasting his time, because he would never go to heaven.

My young friend looked at me with disappointment in his countenance and said nothing. I immediately realized I had made a mistake. You simply do not say things like that about your boss, especially to his son! Although I did not apologize, I wished I had not made that statement. I kept Leister Jr. and Bruce busy and entertained for the rest of the day, hoping they would forget what I had said.

To my surprise and dismay, they ran to their father as soon as he came home from work. They said, "Daddy, Daddy, you know what? Eddie said you will never go to heaven!"

I thought I had lost my job.

Leister did not say anything right away. He waited until later, when I was clearing the dishes from the table after dinner. Then he calmly said, "Eddie, I believe you said I won't go to heaven. Why?"

After stammering and fumbling for words, I reminded him that he once told me that he had killed someone in a war. I said, "The Bible says, 'Thou shalt not kill.' And you killed."

In response to my accusation, Leister took time to help me understand that he had fought in the war to protect his family and friends. He also reminded me that the ancient Israelites in the Bible sometimes had to fight for similar reasons. "It's different in those situations," he said. "When you're required to defend your country, it's different."

That impressed me.

Leister must have sensed that I felt something, because he changed the subject and asked if I was going to any church. I said I wasn't but that I used to attend the Roman Catholic Church. Leister nodded, handed me a copy of the Book of Mormon, and asked me to read it.

I took the book and placed it on a little table in my room. With the angel Moroni shining in gold on the hard cover, the book was an attractive addition to the place. I dusted it occasionally but never read it. Leister asked me periodically, "Are you reading that book?" I always lied and said I was. I was happy that I still had my job, but I had no interest in reading the Book of Mormon.

The Book on the Table

One Sunday morning, I got up, showered, dressed, and had breakfast. My friends were out of town, so I was compelled to break from our normal Sunday routine. As I thought about what to do, I looked down and saw the Book of Mormon on my table. Reluctantly, I picked up the book and walked outside. I went to a railroad line outside the township, sat down, and began reading.

At that time in my life, my reading comprehension in English was limited. Although I was interested in the Book of Mormon, I started dozing whenever I tried to read it. But I had a positive impression of Joseph Smith's testimony at the beginning of the book, so I frequently reread that portion. And even though my understanding of the rest of the book was very limited, I felt good about what I was reading.

Over the next weeks and months, I felt a burning desire to continue reading, and so I did. As a result, I began to see things more clearly. The words in the Book of Mormon were soothing to me—and more than that, I felt their reality and truthfulness. It

Studying the Book of Mormon—a lifelong effort

was as if I had experienced this overwhelming joy before. I sensed a familiar feeling from somewhere in a distant but real past.

What I didn't realize at the time was that I was becoming converted to the restored gospel of the Lord Jesus Christ, through the power of His word.

Discovering the Simple Good News of Christ

One of the passages that touched me was the account of Jesus Christ appearing to the Nephites, recorded in 3 Nephi. The story resonated with me because I had learned of the Savior as a little boy—from family members and from my experiences in the Catholic Church. It also resonated with me because the Savior came down from heaven after the people experienced political upheaval, war, class distinctions, tribalism, and corruption (see 3 Nephi 1–7). When I read this account, my country had been suffering similar trials. Three years earlier, we had fought to obtain independence from Great Britain. We were still emerging from that lengthy and brutal war. The war had claimed thousands of lives and had left others maimed for life. Some of the dead and injured were people I knew.

Because of these personal experiences, I felt a connection with the Nephites. I marveled that the Savior visited them in their time of turmoil, and I felt the comfort and peace they must have felt when He invited them to thrust their hands into His side and feel the nail prints in His hands and feet. I still remember how I felt when I read this passage:

"Behold, I am Jesus Christ, whom the prophets testified shall come into the world. And behold, I am the light and the life of the world. . . . Arise and come forth unto me, that ye may thrust your hands into my side, and also that ye may feel the prints of the nails in my hands and in my feet, that ye may know that I am the God of Israel, and the God of the whole earth, and have been slain for the sins of the world" (3 Nephi 11:10–11, 14).

These words flowed into me with a warmth that enlightened my mind. I felt close to the Lord Jesus Christ. I felt as though I was among those He had retrieved from the human heap of despair. This knowledge and experience gave me a calm sense of worth.

I was discovering the simple good news of Jesus Christ.

A New Testimony

Now I began feeling that I should go to church. I knew where the Latter-day Saint meetinghouse was in my city, and I even knew a few of the people who worshipped there. By this time, Leister Heath and his family had moved out of the country, but Leister had introduced me to John Hove Newbold, a leader in the branch, and his wife, Jean. I worked for the Newbolds.

Despite my persistent feelings about the Church and my friendship with Church members, I didn't immediately gather enough courage to attend a Sunday meeting. My personal fears and perceptions held me back.

For the next few Sundays, I stood a safe distance from the meetinghouse and watched those who entered the chapel. I felt inadequate. I worried that I would not fit in with them. All of them were white, and many of them drove vehicles. The men dressed in white shirts and ties, and some even wore dark suits. I reasoned that I probably needed to wait at least until I could purchase a white shirt and a tie.

Somehow, my friends Jean and John noticed me and saw my timid interest. They asked if I wanted to learn more about the Church. When I told Jean about my experience with the Book of Mormon, she encouraged me to go to a Sunday meeting, even before I had a white shirt and tie. I gradually gathered courage to walk into that building.

On February 5, 1984, at the age of 21, I finally entered the Kwekwe chapel of The Church of Jesus Christ of Latter-day Saints. When I did so, I immediately wanted to walk right back out. I was uncomfortable, feeling that I was in a servant relationship to most of those in attendance. But I stayed and sat down on the back row.

My friend Leister had been replaced by a new branch president, a man named Mike Allen. As the meeting progressed, President Allen bore witness of the Savior Jesus Christ and the Book of Mormon. Then he invited people in the congregation to share their witnesses of the truth. Two members stood and expressed their faith in the Savior Jesus Christ and testified of the truthfulness of the Book of Mormon. As I listened, I began to feel that I could connect with these people. Their words brought comfort and peace to my mind.

Suddenly I found myself on my feet. Yes, I was the fourth person to speak in the meeting. I said, "I too am reading the Book of Mormon. I like it, and I love Jesus Christ. Thank you." Then I quickly sat down.

After the meeting, a few members approached me and said I was welcome in the Church. Sister Newbold told me about Sunday School, and I attended that class. Then a brother in the branch invited me to go to priesthood meeting. Another member told me of a class on Tuesday night that I could attend to learn more about the gospel. I felt overwhelmed by the love of these Saints.

For a while, I would continue to struggle with doubts about whether I belonged at church. But I had learned something that would sustain me in those times of doubt. I learned that we can always find comfort in the Lord's word. And we can receive more than comfort. We can receive strength—strength to do things we have never imagined we could do.

The gate of heaven is open unto all, even to those who will believe on the name of Jesus Christ, who is the Son of God.

Yea, we see that whosoever will may lay hold upon the word of God, which is quick and powerful, which shall divide asunder all the cunning and the snares and the wiles of the devil, and lead the man of Christ in a strait and narrow course across that everlasting gulf of misery which is prepared to engulf the wicked—

And land their souls, yea, their immortal souls, at the right hand of God in the kingdom of heaven.

HELAMAN 3:28–30

CHAPTER 6

Our Divine Nature and Destiny

After my first experience in a sacrament meeting, I started learning from members of the branch. I listened closely to the lessons they taught, and I read the Book of Mormon. I continued to attend church, but I also continued to struggle with feeling that I was inferior to the members of the Kwekwe Branch. I wondered if I belonged among those people who called themselves Saints.

A Powerful Idea

My doubts about myself began to fade one Sunday when all the children in the branch stood in front of the congregation and gave a special presentation. Those little children taught me something. They sang a song I had never heard before:

> *I am a child of God,*
> *And he has sent me here. . . .*
> *I am a child of God,*
> *And so my needs are great. . . .*
> *I am a child of God,*
> *Rich blessings are in store.*[8]

As I looked at the faces of those children and listened to them sing, I felt the words of their song lift me above the dust of the world. I realized for the first time that I was a son of God and that He had a plan for me.

This song gave me courage to progress toward baptism. Why did a little Primary song have such a profound impact on me? Because it helped me see what God saw in me. He saw me as His child, endowed with the great potential to become like Him.

President Dallin H. Oaks observed: "Consider the power of the idea taught in our beloved song 'I Am a Child of God.' . . . Here is the answer to one of life's great questions, 'Who am I?' I am a child of God with a spirit lineage to heavenly parents. That parentage defines our eternal potential. That powerful idea is a potent antidepressant. It can strengthen each of us to make righteous choices and to seek the best that is within us. Establish in the mind of a young person the powerful idea that he or she is a child of God and you have given self-respect and motivation to move against the problems of life."[9]

I had been worried about whether I belonged with the members of the branch. This song helped me connect with them, but it did more than that. It inspired me to connect with my Father in Heaven, to begin to see what He saw in me.

I had been like Moses, who, as a humble shepherd, asked the very question President Oaks mentioned: "Who am I?" When the Lord appeared to Moses in a burning bush and commanded him to deliver the covenant people from Egypt, Moses said, "Who am I, that I should go unto Pharaoh, and that I should bring forth the children of Israel out of Egypt?" (Exodus 3:11).

The Lord replied, "Certainly I will be with thee" (Exodus 3:12). He also repeatedly called Moses "my son" (Moses 1:4, 6,

7, 40). With this assurance, Moses was able to withstand temptation when Satan came to distract him from his calling. Satan said, "Moses, son of man, worship me." Moses replied, "Behold, I am a son of God, in the similitude of his Only Begotten; and where is thy glory, that I should worship thee?" (Moses 1:12–13).

This powerful idea—that we are sons and daughters of God—opens our eyes to our divine nature and destiny. It helps us see that we can become like our Heavenly Father.

We learn this truth from apostles and prophets and from the Holy Ghost, who testifies of their teachings. In Athens, the Apostle Paul testified, "We are the offspring of God" (Acts 17:29). In an epistle to the Romans, he taught: "The Spirit itself beareth witness with our spirit, that we are the children of God: And if children, then heirs; heirs of God, and joint-heirs with Christ; if so be that we suffer with him, that we may be also glorified together" (Romans 8:16–17).

We also learn this truth from Jesus Christ Himself, the One who makes it all possible. To a group of people who accused Him of blasphemy because He declared that He was God's Son, He referred to a psalm in the Old Testament and declared, "Is it not written in your law, I said, Ye are gods"? (John 10:34; see also Psalm 82:6). In a revelation to John the Beloved, He promised, "To him that overcometh will I grant to sit with me in my throne, even as I also overcame, and am set down with my Father in his throne" (Revelation 3:21). And in this dispensation, He revealed that those who are true to the everlasting covenant "shall . . . be gods, because they have no end" (Doctrine and Covenants 132:20).

Children, Not Creations

This might seem like an impossible task and an unimaginable philosophy, but not if we really think about the words I heard the children sing in the Kwekwe Branch: "I am a child of God." Elder Tad R. Callister pointed out that many people "believe that we are the spirit creations of God, just as a building is the creation of its architect or a painting the creation of its painter or an invention the creation of its inventor. The scriptures, however, teach a much different doctrine. They teach that we are more than creations of God; they teach that we are the literal spirit offspring of God our Father. Paul taught this truth in unequivocal terms: 'We are the offspring of God' (Acts 17:29)."

Elder Callister asked, "Why is this distinction important?" Then he answered his own question: "The difference is monumental in its consequence because our identity determines in large measure our destiny. For example, can a mere creation ever become like its creator? Can a building ever become an architect? A painting a painter? Or an invention an inventor?"[10]

The answer to these questions is, of course, no. But children can become like their parents. God's children can become gods. What does this mean? I don't completely know. I do know that we have a divine destiny because of our divine parentage. As I consider what this means, I think about my earthly father. I resemble him in my height and in the way I talk, and I have become a father myself. But I will never be the father of my father. So it is with our relationship with our Heavenly Father. We will never be gods of our God, but "through the Atonement of Jesus

Christ, God can exalt all His children—meaning empower them to become like Him."[11]

Pressing Forward with Faith in Christ

Inspired by this vision, I am motivated to follow Paul's example and "press toward the mark for the prize of the high calling of God." I know that what Paul said is true: this is possible only "in Christ Jesus" (Philippians 3:14). As I said earlier, the idea of becoming like God might seem like an impossible task and an unimaginable philosophy. It *would* be impossible and unimaginable without our Savior and His atoning power. We need His miracle of forgiveness. We need His sustaining grace.

Elder David A. Bednar taught: "We will not attain a state of perfection in this life, but we can and should press forward with faith in Christ along the strait and narrow path and make steady progress toward our eternal destiny. The Lord's pattern for spiritual development is 'line upon line, precept upon precept, here a little and there a little' (2 Nephi 28:30). Small, steady, incremental spiritual improvements are the steps the Lord would have us take. Preparing to walk guiltless before God is one of the primary purposes of mortality and the pursuit of a lifetime; it does not result from sporadic spurts of intense spiritual activity. . . . The Savior will strengthen and assist us to make sustained, paced progress."[12]

Belonging

After hearing "I Am a Child of God" for the first time, I held my head high as I walked home from church. I sensed that I really did belong in The Church of Jesus Christ of Latter-day Saints. I knew God loved me, and I felt that He had a great work for me to

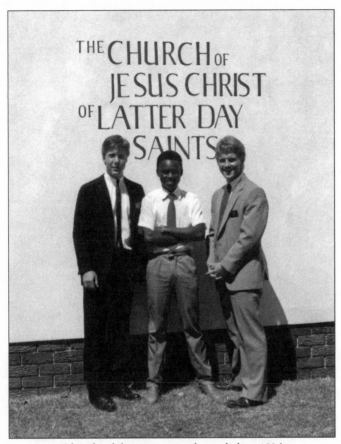

Edward and the missionaries who taught him, 1984:
Russell Grifiths, left, and James H. Hall, right

do in His kingdom. I was beginning to see myself as He saw me, and I was preparing to walk in His covenant path.

Not long after that, on August 18, 1984, I wanted my family and friends to share in the truths I had learned. I walked through my neighborhood, inviting people to come to my baptismal service the next day. And on August 19, at the age of 22, I was baptized by Brother John Newbold and confirmed a member of The Church of Jesus Christ of Latter-day Saints by President Mike

Allen. My missionaries, Elders Russell Griffiths and James Hall, looked on joyfully.

I was beginning my journey in the Lord's earthly kingdom—a journey toward the divine potential my Heavenly Father and my Savior saw in me. I know They see this potential in all of us.

> Grace and peace be multiplied unto you through the knowledge of God, and of Jesus our Lord, according as his divine power hath given unto us all things that pertain unto life and godliness, through the knowledge of him that hath called us to glory and virtue:
>
> Whereby are given unto us exceeding great and precious promises: that by these ye might be partakers of the divine nature.
>
> 2 PETER 1:2–4

CHAPTER 7

Like an Awakening Dawn

"I stand all amazed at the love Jesus offers me."[13] I heard this hymn for the first time when I finally found the courage to attend a sacrament meeting of The Church of Jesus Christ of Latter-day Saints. The message of the hymn was familiar. It was similar to a thought I frequently had as a child when I sat in our Catholic chapel: "Hey! He really went through a lot . . . just for me!"[14]

The ordinance of the sacrament was also somewhat familiar, like the Catholic communion I remembered from my childhood. But I noticed one thing that was very different: young men administered that sacred ordinance. Their reverence and dignity touched my heart. I felt that something important was about to happen, and I was right. I was about to begin a journey that would lead me to join those young men in the administration of the sacrament.

Several months later, I was a new convert and a recently ordained priest. The branch president, Mike Allen, approached me at church one day. He asked me to become familiar with the sacrament prayers so I could administer the sacrament the next

Sunday. I was overwhelmed and anxious. I read and reread the prayers that week, almost committing them to memory. I felt responsible, respectful, and aware that I would be praying on behalf of the whole branch.

When I knelt before the congregation to pray the next Sunday, my anxiety melted away. I felt a calm sense of worth. The words of the sacrament prayer touched my senses like an awakening dawn, enlightening and uplifting me. Joy overwhelmed me, encompassing my thoughts and enfolding my mind in peace. Never before had my comprehension of the goodness of the Savior reached such heights.

Sacrifice and Sacrament

Since those early days, the ordinance of the sacrament has continued to bring deep meaning to my life. My understanding has deepened as I have pondered the connection between sacrifice and sacrament.

Heavenly Father has always required His children to offer sacrifices as a form of worship. Beginning with Adam and Eve and extending to the time of the Savior's mortal ministry, animal sacrifices pointed to the atoning sacrifice of the Lamb of God. But just before Jesus Christ carried out that atoning sacrifice, He met with His Apostles in an upper room for a Passover meal. Jesus "took bread, and gave thanks, and brake it, and gave unto them, saying, This is my body which is given for you: this do in remembrance of me. Likewise also the cup after supper, saying, This cup is the new testament in my blood, which is shed for you" (Luke 22:19–20). He instituted the sacrament—a priesthood ordinance to replace animal sacrifices.

Soon after the Savior carried out His atoning sacrifice, the Saints in the Western Hemisphere heard Him speak of a new sacrifice that He required of them. "Ye shall offer up unto me no more the shedding of blood," He said. "Yea, your sacrifices and your burnt offerings shall be done away, for I will accept none of your sacrifices and your burnt offerings. And ye shall offer for a sacrifice unto me a broken heart and a contrite spirit" (3 Nephi 9:19–20). That same day, He instituted the sacrament among the Nephites. He taught: "This shall ye do in remembrance of my body, which I have shown unto you. And it shall be a testimony unto the Father that ye do always remember me. And if ye do always remember me ye shall have my Spirit to be with you" (3 Nephi 18:7).

This is our promise when we partake of the sacrament. Our participation in the ordinance is "a testimony unto the Father that [we] do always remember [the Son]" (3 Nephi 18:7). It represents our sacrifice of a broken heart and a contrite spirit. As Elder D. Todd Christofferson taught, "As you seek the blessing of conversion, you can offer the Lord the gift of your broken, or repentant, heart and your contrite, or obedient, spirit. In reality, it is the gift of yourself—what you are and what you are becoming."[15]

Remembering the Savior's Suffering

I am grateful for the way the sacrament helps me turn to my Savior and come unto Him. When I partake of the sacrament, there are a few things I always try to remember about Him.

The Savior's Institution of the Sacrament

Each time I partake of the sacrament, I reflect on the occasion when the Savior asked Peter and John to go and prepare for the Passover (see Luke 22:7–13). I wonder how those Apostles felt. They did not understand everything Jesus was about to do, but they and their brethren in the Twelve must have sensed that this was not a typical Passover meal. I wonder how they felt "when the hour was come [and] he sat down, and the twelve apostles with him," and when He said, "With desire I have desired to eat this passover with you before I suffer" (Luke 22:14–15).

What would He suffer? They could not have known. Today we can look back with some knowledge of His suffering, even though we will never comprehend it.

The Garden of Gethsemane

When I partake of the sacrament, I think about the Savior in the Garden of Gethsemane. We know that soon after He instituted the sacrament, His suffering began there (see Matthew 26:36–38). Luke recorded: "And he was withdrawn from them about a stone's cast, and kneeled down, and prayed, saying, Father, if thou be willing, remove this cup from me: nevertheless not my will, but thine, be done. . . . And being in an agony he prayed more earnestly: and he sweat as it were great drops of blood falling down to the ground" (Luke 22:41–42; Joseph Smith Translation, Luke 22:44).

Jesus Christ Himself described His experience in Gethsemane. Referring to His suffering, He said: "How sore you know not, how exquisite you know not, yea, how hard to bear you know not. . . . I, God, have suffered these things for all . . . ; which suffering caused myself, even God, the greatest of all, to tremble because of pain, and to bleed at every pore, and to suffer both body and spirit—and would that I might not drink the bitter cup, and shrink" (Doctrine and Covenants 19:15–16, 18).

Sleeping Disciples

When I partake of the sacrament, I often think about Peter, James, and John sleeping while the Savior suffered (see Matthew

26:37–45). Then I ask myself about my standing before Him. What do I refuse to give up that is keeping me from being able to "do all things through Christ which strengtheneth me"? (Philippians 4:13). Why do I sometimes fail to see my potential as He sees it? When the time comes for me to stand before Him and He looks into my soul with His loving, searching eyes, will I be able to look directly back at Him? Or will He ask me, as He asked Peter, James, and John, "Why sleep ye?" (see Luke 22:46). Will He ask, "Why do you not receive my help to fulfill your divine destiny?"

The Strenuous Road to Golgotha

When I partake of the sacrament, I think about the Savior's strenuous road to Golgotha after He left Gethsemane: "Then took they him, and led him, and brought him into the high priest's house. . . . And the men that held Jesus mocked him, and smote him. And when they had blindfolded him, they struck him on the face, and asked him, saying, Prophesy, who is it that smote thee? And many other things blasphemously spake they against him" (Luke 22:54, 63–65). And later: "Pilate . . . , willing to release Jesus, spake again to them. But they cried, saying, Crucify him, crucify him" (Luke 23:20–21).

Selflessness in the Face of Selfishness

When I partake of the sacrament, I think of the Savior's selfless sacrifice on the cross, even when so many around Him were selfish. "And when they were come to the place, which is called Calvary, there they crucified him, and the malefactors, one on the right hand, and the other on the left. . . . And one of the malefactors which were hanged railed on him, saying, If thou be Christ, save thyself and us. But the other answering rebuked him, saying, Dost not thou fear God, seeing thou art in the same condemnation? And we indeed justly; for we receive the due reward of our deeds: but this man hath done nothing amiss. And he said unto Jesus, Lord, remember me when thou comest into thy kingdom" (Luke 23:33, 39–42).

As I think about these people—the high priest and Pilate and the people who demanded that Jesus be crucified and the malefactor who railed against Jesus—I hope I will never let selfish desires blind me from knowing my Savior. I hope I will always remember His selfless sacrifice, receive His grace, and acknowledge His hand in my life. I hope I will, like the second malefactor, be humble enough to acknowledge Him and plead for Him to remember me.

With such humility comes the Lord's assurance and promise: "Behold, I, God, have suffered these things for all, that they might not suffer if they would repent; . . . Glory be to the Father, and I partook and finished my preparations unto the children of men" (Doctrine and Covenants 19:16, 19).

Sacrament, Self-Examination, Repentance, Forgiveness, and Personal Revelation

The sacrament is a time of self-examination and repentance. It is a time to acknowledge our weakness and our need for the Lord to cleanse us and "make [us] a new heart and a new spirit" (Ezekiel 18:31). In our efforts to make changes in our lives and make a difference in the lives of others, we need Him. Only through Him and His Atonement can we find lasting success and joy. Only "through the shedding of the blood of Christ, which is in the covenant of the Father unto the remission of [our] sins," can we "become holy, without spot" (Moroni 10:33). He is "the way, the truth, and the life" (John 14:6). I am grateful for the sacrament—for the simple way it reminds me of the price Jesus Christ has paid so we can repent, receive forgiveness, and become like Him.

Our experience with the sacrament can also lead to personal revelation. The promise in the sacrament prayers is that we will always have the Spirit to be with us (see Doctrine and Covenants 20:77, 79). Sometimes when we least expect it, maybe during the administration of the sacrament or during a talk in the meeting or on our way home from church, the Holy Ghost sheds light on questions we have and difficulties we face.

Partaking of the sacrament is a privilege. As we partake worthily and thoughtfully, our weekly experience can be like my experience the first time I pronounced the blessings on the bread and water. And it can remain with us, lasting beyond the few minutes of the ordinance. We can feel a calm sense of worth. The words of the sacrament prayer can touch our senses like an awakening dawn, enlightening and uplifting us again and again. We can be encompassed about with joy and peace, and our understanding of the Savior's goodness can continue to grow. We will surely have His Spirit to be with us, and we will see ourselves, more and more, as God sees us.

As they were eating, Jesus took bread and brake it, and blessed it, and gave to his disciples, and said, Take, eat; this is in remembrance of my body which I give a ransom for you. . . .

For this is in remembrance of my blood of the new testament, which is shed for as many as shall believe on my name, for the remission of their sins.

JOSEPH SMITH TRANSLATION, MATTHEW 26:22, 24

CHAPTER 8

Courage to Testify

I love fast and testimony meetings. When I share my testimony, I give what I have. And as I strive to strengthen others, my testimony grows stronger. I have learned the truth of what President Boyd K. Packer taught: "A testimony is to be *found* in the *bearing* of it! . . . It is one thing to receive a witness from what you have read or what another has said; and that is a necessary beginning. It is quite another to have the Spirit confirm to you in your bosom that what *you* have testified is true. . . . As you give that which you have, there is a replacement, with increase!"[16]

A Difficult Challenge

My first experience in a fast and testimony meeting was a dramatic turning point in my life (see chapter 5 in this book). I felt the influence of the Spirit without even knowing what I was feeling, and I stood and shared what I was beginning to know. Doubts that had existed in my heart vanished. I made up my mind that day that I wanted to belong to The Church of Jesus Christ of Latter-day Saints.

After that initial fast and testimony meeting experience, I looked forward to another meeting each month. I always fasted and took the opportunity to bear my testimony. Because English is my second language, I struggled to express myself in my English-speaking branch, so I wrote my testimony on a piece of paper and read it to my fellow Saints.

I had been writing and reading my testimony for a few months when my branch president, Mike Allen, called me into his office. He gently told me that a testimony is a spiritual witness given by the Holy Ghost. He admonished me to prepare myself spiritually, listen to the impressions I received, and share those impressions in the very moment rather than write down my testimony as a talk. He reminded me of my first day at church when I stood and testified without written notes. He encouraged me to continue with that kind of faith—to bear my testimony from the heart.

I told President Allen that I would accept his invitation. What I did not tell him was that it would be a tremendous challenge. It was difficult for me to write in English, but it was even more difficult for me to express myself aloud without written notes.

In preparation for the next fast Sunday, I wrote my testimony and memorized it. In our fast and testimony meeting, I walked to the pulpit and stood there without saying anything for a minute that felt like an eternity. I couldn't remember the words I had memorized. Finally, when I found the strength to speak, my words were haphazard and meaningless in my own mind. The congregation looked at me strangely. I felt terrible.

After that experience, I resolved never to bear my testimony again. I did not want to embarrass myself. Instead, I sat and listened carefully to the testimonies of my brothers and sisters in the branch. I felt their spiritual witnesses of the Savior and of Joseph

Smith's First Vision. I was inspired by each affirmation that the Book of Mormon teaches and testifies of Jesus Christ.

Bearing Testimony from the Heart

After a while, my motivation to share my own testimony returned. With each succeeding fast and testimony meeting, this desire welled up inside me in a new and more compelling way. My soul was hungry for spiritual nourishment. I was like a starving man, but the nourishment I sought could come only from inside myself, as the Lord inspired me.

Still, I fought the urge to share my testimony for months. But one fast Sunday as the meeting was about to end, I couldn't hold back. I stood where I was and declared my own witness of the Savior. I was able to "declare the things which [I had] heard, and verily believe, and know to be true" (Doctrine and Covenants 80:4). My own sincere expressions were mellow and soothing to me. More than that—they rang true. I couldn't adequately express my feelings. It was as if I had experienced such joy somewhere before in a dim past, and now it had returned, even stronger. I felt the Lord's love for me, and I wanted to be better.

Strengthening Others and Ourselves

I knew then, as I know now, that I should share my testimony as a service to others. Bearing testimony to others can be frightening, but even our simple words, if they come from our hearts and are guided by the Spirit, have power to change lives.

I also knew then, as I know now, that I receive personal blessings when I share my testimony. About a year after the Church was organized in these latter days, the Lord revealed the following truth through the Prophet Joseph Smith to a small group of Saints: "Ye are blessed, for the testimony which ye have borne is recorded in heaven for the angels to look upon; and they rejoice over you, and your sins are forgiven you" (Doctrine and Covenants 62:3).

Today I am no longer afraid to share my testimony. I testify of the Savior and His Atonement whenever I have an opportunity. I bear testimony of the Book of Mormon and its prophecies and teachings that have changed my life. I also invite others to share their testimonies—with their children, their parents, their friends, their colleagues, their schoolmates. Through our words and example, the Holy Ghost can strengthen and inspire family, friends, and even strangers. And as President Packer promised, we will receive an increase in the process.

> A commandment I give unto you, that ye shall declare whatsoever thing ye declare in my name, in solemnity of heart, in the spirit of meekness, in all things.
>
> And I give unto you this promise, that inasmuch as ye do this the Holy Ghost shall be shed forth in bearing record unto all things whatsoever ye shall say.
>
> DOCTRINE AND COVENANTS 100:7–8

CHAPTER 9

Not What We Do,
but Who We Become

Toward the end of 1984, when I had been a member of the Church for about four months, President Mike Allen invited me to his office at the meetinghouse of the Kwekwe Branch. As he and I talked, we looked through the window and saw the full-time missionaries playing with branch members outside the building. President Allen said, "Eddie, how would you like to be like those two young missionaries someday?" I answered that I would love to, and I asked what I would need to do to become a missionary.

President Allen said that as a missionary, I would devote most of my time to teaching the gospel of Jesus Christ. "The best way to prepare," he said, "is to become a gospel scholar." He encouraged me to continue studying the scriptures, especially the Book of Mormon, and he gave me a copy of *Truth Restored*, a brief review of Church history. He said that I should take every opportunity to serve with the full-time missionaries. He also said I would need to prepare financially. He reinforced the importance of paying tithing, saving a portion of my earnings, and continuing to pursue an education.

Tragically, not long thereafter, President Allen drowned while tubing in the Sebakwe River near Kwekwe. I was shocked by his death. As I thought about everything he had taught me, I was determined to follow his counsel and do whatever I needed to do to become a missionary. The Lord said, "If ye have desires to serve God ye are called to the work" (Doctrine and Covenants 4:3). I had such desires, and I had faith that He would call me to serve.

Preparing to Serve

I was 22 years old at the time, living alone in a rented room. In addition to paying tithing, supporting myself, and paying for my education, I was providing financial support for the education of my younger brother Cosmos. It would be difficult to save extra money for a mission, but I knew that the Lord saw me as a future missionary. I knew that if I worked hard to prepare for a mission, He would bless me in my efforts.

I was employed as a night watchman at the Church meeting-house. I supplemented my income by riding the train between Kwekwe and Bulawayo, a distance of about 230 kilometers (145 miles), and selling items such as boiled eggs and sweets to passengers. I bought clothes from manufacturers in Bulawayo and brought them back to Kwekwe, where I sold them for a reasonable profit.

After more than a year, I had saved $140, which was a lot of money at that time. John Newbold, who was then serving as branch president, helped me submit my papers so I could be considered as a candidate for missionary service.

While I worked to support myself and my brother, I served with the full-time missionaries as often as I could, especially on the weekends. They often gave me opportunities to participate in the lessons, asking me to teach a principle or share my testimony. Through these efforts and through weekly volleyball games with

Edward (right), just prior to baptizing Jared Machumi, May 12, 1985

the branch, youth and young adults in the neighborhood began to show interest in the Church. A few of them were baptized. So I got a taste of missionary work before I was a full-time missionary.

Learning to Serve

I was called to serve as a full-time missionary at the age of 24. I was assigned to labor in the South Africa Johannesburg Mission, with a specific assignment to preach the gospel of Jesus Christ in my home country of Zimbabwe.

My full-time mission started in Bindura, about 300 kilometers (185 miles) from Kwekwe, on April 1, 1986. There was no Missionary Training Center in South Africa at the time, so my initial training was "on the job." I was not able to go to the Johannesburg South Africa Temple, so I had not yet received the temple endowment. I was not even set apart until three weeks into my mission. But I was an ordained elder, and I had a testimony of the restored gospel and a burning desire to share it.

The Lord blessed me with a wonderful trainer: Elder Robert Hall, from Syracuse, Utah. He taught me how to serve, and he showed me that an important part of our service happens when we are on our knees.

When Elder Hall and I first prayed together, I said the prayer. I was surprised to see that he remained on his knees for what I thought was a long time, even after I had said "amen." I thought

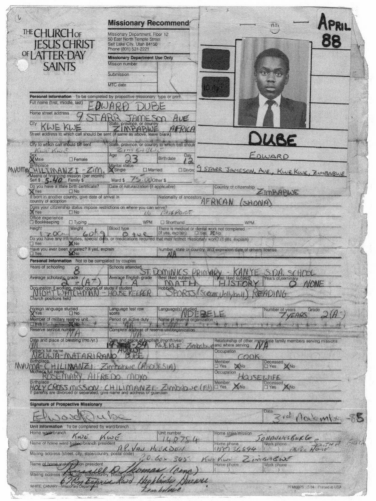

Edward's missionary application and photo, 1986

that maybe I had failed to cover some important things in my prayer. But the next time, he said the prayer, and he did the same thing. He stayed on his knees after I thought the prayer was over.

This pattern continued for a while until finally I couldn't take it anymore. While he was still on his knees after one prayer, I asked him what he was doing down there. He did not respond immediately. When he did respond, he taught me a lesson of a lifetime.

Elder Hall said that at the end of each day, he reflected on what he had done. He let his mind capture the events of the day—things he could have done better and times when he felt the hand of the Lord. He asked for forgiveness for his shortcomings and expressed gratitude for the blessings he had received.

Since that day, I have tried to follow Elder Hall's example—a pattern we can all follow to become the people God wants us to become. Each night, I strive to pray with real intent and to listen to the Spirit. I evaluate my service that day and report to my Heavenly Father. I thank Him for His blessings and for the times He has used me as an instrument in His hands. I ask Him to forgive me of my sins and shortcomings. And I listen for His response, through the whisperings of the Holy Ghost. This practice greatly blesses my life. I go to bed renewed and enjoy the peace of knowing that I am in good standing with my Heavenly Father. Each morning, I wake up ready to serve again.

In those first days of my mission—without a missionary training center, before I received the temple endowment, even before I was set apart as a missionary—I received one of my greatest, most lasting lessons about prayer and service. Elder Robert Hall helped me open my eyes a little bit more to see what God saw in me—and what God sees in all His children. I learned, more than I had realized before, that Heavenly Father really does listen to our prayers. As I applied my heart in prayer, I felt, more than I had felt before, Jesus Christ's redeeming power in my life. I wanted to help others experience His power. Rather than focusing on what I needed to *do* each day, I thought about what I could *become* each day and how I could be an instrument in the hands of the Lord. I was ready for the Lord to expand my vision.

> If ye will enter in by the way, and receive the Holy Ghost, it will show unto you all things what ye should do. . . .
>
> Behold, I say unto you that ye must pray always, and not faint; that ye must not perform any thing unto the Lord save in the first place ye shall pray unto the Father in the name of Christ, that he will consecrate thy performance unto thee, that thy performance may be for the welfare of thy soul.
>
> 2 NEPHI 32:5, 9

PART II

EXPANDING OUR VISION

When that which is perfect is come,
then that which is in part shall be done away. . . .

Now I know in part; but then shall I know
even as also I am known.

1 CORINTHIANS 13:10, 12

CHAPTER 10

The Design of Our God

When I left home as a missionary, I knew I would be an instrument in the Lord's hands to help others come to the knowledge of His restored gospel. I also knew the experience would strengthen me as His disciple. I had no idea what joy and pain would come as I learned to live as His servant. In a way, I was like a group of Latter-day Saints who met together in Jackson County, Missouri, on August 1, 1831. Less than two weeks before this meeting, the Lord had revealed to the Prophet Joseph Smith, "This is the land of promise, and the place for the city of Zion." He had said that the city of Independence, Missouri, would be "the center place," where a temple would stand (Doctrine and Covenants 57:2–3).

That little group of Saints must have been full of joyful anticipation for the days and years ahead. They gathered in a land of promise—their Zion. How do you think they felt when the Lord revealed the following words on that day? "Ye cannot behold with your natural eyes, for the present time, the design of your God concerning those things which shall come hereafter, and the glory which shall follow after much tribulation" (Doctrine and Covenants 58:3).

What glory awaited them? What tribulation would they endure? Within two years, they would be forced from Jackson County, their homes in flames. They would not build their temple in Independence. But three years after that, many of them would gather in the Kirtland Temple, where the Lord "manifest[ed] himself" to them so His servants could "go forth . . . armed with [His] power" (Doctrine and Covenants 109:5, 22). Two years after that, the Saints in Kirtland would be forced to abandon their homes. After another year, they would be driven from the state of Missouri while the Prophet Joseph Smith, his brother Hyrum, and a few faithful friends suffered in jail. The Saints would also experience tribulation and glory in Nauvoo: the establishment of a beautiful city, continuing persecution and dissension, a growing covenant community, the martyrdom of Joseph and Hyrum, a majestic temple where they would receive ordinances of exaltation, and an exodus to the wilderness in the west. More tribulation would follow—and more glory—and more temples. Ultimately, they could be "crowned with much glory" (Doctrine and Covenants 58:4)—the blessings of exaltation.

But on August 1, 1831, the Saints in Jackson County could not have foreseen the price they would pay or the blessings they would receive. They could not have beheld God's design in the things they would experience—His design for them and for those who would follow in their footsteps. The Lord's words to those Latter-day Saints were true for me when I started my mission. They are true for all of us. We "cannot behold with [our] natural eyes, for the present time, the design of [our] God concerning those things which shall come hereafter, and the glory which shall follow after much tribulation."

Learning about God's Design

Toward the end of my service as a full-time missionary, when I was 26 years old, a series of experiences helped me learn about God's design for my life.

These experiences began in the Famona Branch, in Bulawayo, Zimbabwe, where my companion was Elder Tangisai Nyanhamo. This was my second time serving in the branch, a place that had been difficult for missionary work for many years. The Caucasian and native African members were experiencing a difficult transition after Zimbabwe gained independence from Great Britain. They had not associated with each other in the past, and they struggled to join together in a circle of friendship.

Some members who had been in the Church for a number of years had missed out on the rewarding opportunity to help

Bulawayo missionaries, 1988. Left to right: Tangisai Nyanhamo, Raphael Chibota, Frances Jack, and Edward Dube

new converts and people who were being taught by missionaries. Rather than fully embracing new and potential members and helping them learn the gospel of Jesus Christ, they seemed more interested in protecting areas of the chapel where they had sat over the years. Because of lingering discomfort about race, they had not yet learned to share simple acts of kindness or invitations to "come and see, come and help, and come and stay."[17]

In the midst of all this, our mission president, Joseph Hamstead, extended a call to a brother named Mark Fraser to serve as branch president. My companion and I were shocked. Brother Fraser, from Great Britain, had rarely talked with anyone, especially not with us missionaries. We wondered what President Hamstead was thinking. We thought the Famona Branch would collapse. We did not see God's design in the calling of this new branch president, and we did not see how it would bless us in the work.

The Sunday after President Fraser was set apart, he invited Elder Nyanhamo and me to come to his office. When we arrived, he asked how we were doing with our missionary work.

Arrogantly, I said, "We don't report to you. We report to our mission president."

President Fraser calmly replied, "I know you don't report to me." Then he said something that startled and humbled us: "You know, I've been watching you. You are the hardest-working missionaries I have ever seen. You work hard." He told us about his vision for missionary work in the branch, and he said he needed our help.

I had mistaken Mark Fraser as a prideful man. He was just a quiet man. But when he was set apart as branch president, he changed. He humbly and boldly rallied the members around missionary work. He often took my companion and me to visit less-active members. Members of the branch joined in the effort. Under President Fraser's leadership, attendance and activity increased. Members embraced each other as brothers and sisters. Together, they drew closer to the Lord, who "inviteth them all to come unto him and partake of his goodness [and] denieth none that come unto him, black and white, bond and free, male and female" (2 Nephi 26:33). The branch was transformed, and my companion and I enjoyed success in leading people to the waters of baptism.

At this time, just before I was to complete my two-year mission, President Hamstead asked me to extend my service for three months. I readily accepted the opportunity, and I wrote to my family to tell them that I would not be returning home as soon as we had planned. The only family member who responded to the news was my brother Onismo. He told me that he had waited for me at the bus stop and had been disappointed that he didn't see me. But he later read my letter and was pleased that I was doing the Lord's work.

At one point in those three additional months of my mission, Elder Nyanhamo and I went to a zone conference in Harare, which was four and a half hours away from the Famona Branch but only ten minutes from where my father was working. One morning I woke up and felt the Spirit prompting me to call my father. In those days, we were allowed to call home only twice a year, so the other missionaries in the apartment advised me not to make the call. I ignored them, picked up the phone, and called. When my father heard my voice, he said that he didn't want to disturb me in my service but that he had something to tell me. My brother Onismo had recently died, drowned in a river.

I was devastated. Since my father was so close by, Elder Brian

Donnelly asked our mission president for permission to visit him. President Hamstead granted permission, and we went to my father's workplace right away.

Onismo fetching firewood for Edward's mission farewell party, April 3, 1986

As soon as I set my eyes on my father, I started crying uncontrollably. I felt empty, heartbroken, lost, and depressed. But my father pointed at my missionary name tag and said, "Edward, accept the Lord's will. You need to accept the things you cannot change and work hard to change those things you can change." He had lost a son, and yet he reached out to me, his son who had left home to serve the Lord. In two sentences, my father, who was not a member of the Church, taught me what I had been trying to teach for two years.

Even after hearing that gentle rebuke, I struggled with pain, sadness, and doubt. As soon as Elder Donnelly and I returned to the mission home in Harare, I started packing my belongings so I could go home. I reasoned that if I had gone home on my official release date, my brother Onismo would not have died.

Before I could go through with my plan to leave the mission, President Hamstead came to see me. He put his arm around my shoulders and said, "Elder Dube, your mission is not over until it is over." He was right, of course. I had no authority to release myself from my mission. As my ecclesiastical leader, only he could do that, and he instead encouraged me to focus on my purpose as a missionary and go to work.

For other missionaries in other trying circumstances, an early release might have been consistent with the Lord's will. President Hamstead knew that for me, the best thing was to stay on my mission. And so I followed the combined counsel of my father and President Hamstead. I completed my mission—all 27 months of it. I am truly grateful for two men who saw who I was and who I could become.

As I followed their counsel, I learned to keep my head up, no matter what situation I might be in. I learned to put my trust in the Lord, who sees the big picture—a picture I cannot see with my natural eyes or comprehend with my limited understanding.

Blessings through Service

I have learned this lesson again and again. Each time I have received a new calling or assignment, I have seen it as part of a journey to follow the Lord and help others follow Him. Each time I have been released, I have joyfully accepted the release, knowing that the journey continues.

On this journey, I have seen that service blesses the giver as well as the receiver. Of course, our reason for giving service is to strengthen others and to help them draw nearer to the Lord. His words to Oliver Cowdery and David Whitmer are true for us: "By your hands I will work a marvelous work among the children of men" (Doctrine and Covenants 18:44). But in this process, He also works a marvelous work within us individually. President Henry B. Eyring taught, "It is serving God and others persistently with full heart and soul that turns testimony of truth into unbreakable spiritual strength."[18]

I see this in the lives of missionaries throughout the world and in the lives of Latter-day Saints of all ages who serve in branches, wards, stakes, and temples. I see it in simple acts of service and in large acts of humanitarian aid. Each minute, hour, day, week, month, and year we serve, the Lord is mindful of us. He never lets us down. I rejoice to be part of His great work and to witness the unfolding of the Restoration of His gospel.

As we serve others, we draw nearer to Jesus Christ. We do not fully grasp what we are becoming—we cannot behold His designs with our natural eyes. But eventually, if we have truly followed Him and allowed ourselves to be filled with His pure love, we will see Him and comprehend His design for our lives. "When he shall appear," Mormon taught, "we shall be like him, for we shall see him as he is" (Moroni 7:48; see also 1 John 3:2).

This is the picture I carry in my mind each day as I look for opportunities to serve others. As I do this, my days are filled with joy, regardless of challenges in my life and in the world around me. I pray as Mormon did: "That we may have this hope; that we may be purified even as he is pure" (Moroni 7:48; see also 1 John 3:3).

The works, and the designs, and the purposes of God
cannot be frustrated, neither can they come to naught.

DOCTRINE AND COVENANTS 3:1

CHAPTER 11

Timely Counsel,
Timeless Blessings

On December 1, 1986, I wrote the following in my missionary journal: "The rain is pouring outside. I could hear rain pounding on the roof as I got up. I lay on my bed with my eyes closed. I thought of my dream. Of course I dreamed of a girl, Naume Salizani."

Before I tell you about the rest of the dream, I should tell you that Naume and her brother Amos were the first people I taught who were baptized. When I arrived in their city of Bindura, they had already begun receiving the missionary discussions. They were baptized a few days after my arrival. I then had the privilege of introducing the gospel to their parents, who also joined the Church.

Back to my dream: "An old lady came to me, pointing to Naume, and said, 'She loves you, can't you see that?' I went to Naume, but I was afraid to talk to her. Why such a dream? I hate to think about girls, for sure, but how can I avoid this? I want to think about my work and to find ways of helping people learn the gospel of Jesus Christ."

Naume, left, with her parents, Anna and Bauleni Salizani. Edward, front, with Tandiwe and Pricilla Salizani, 1988

I did find ways of helping people learn the gospel of Jesus Christ, and I received strength to focus on my purpose as a missionary. For me, Naume was nothing more than a sister in the gospel until I was released from full-time missionary service on July 1, 1988, nineteen months after I had that dream. I was 26 years old at the time of my release.

Today, Naume is still a sister in the gospel, and she is also my eternal companion. That dream was a source of revelation, as dreams sometimes are. The Lord used an old woman—someone who inspired my deep respect—to teach me what He wanted me to know.

But it took more than an old woman in a dream to get Naume and me together. When I was a recently returned missionary with very little money, I worried that I wasn't ready to get married and support a family. It was like I was stuck in the shade of the mango tree again, unwilling to venture past what I knew. Fortunately, my vision expanded as I received counsel from a prophet, a missionary, and a local Church leader, combined with promptings from the Holy Ghost. I learned that great blessings come when we accept the Lord's will and the Lord's timing.

Long-Distance Courtship and Proposal

I began my courtship with Naume shortly after I returned home. Our lack of money and the distance between our homes made it almost impossible for us to meet. I simply could not afford the four-hour bus ride from Kwekwe to Bindura. So we wrote letters to each other.

In our first few letters, we worked to establish a friendship. Our discussion often centered on how her parents and other family members were progressing in the Church. After these letters full of pleasantries, I quickly moved on to the real point, which I had delayed for almost two years since my revelatory dream. I shared my feelings with Naume and proposed marriage to her in a letter.

Naume's response to my letter was very pleasant, but she did not refer to the subject of marriage at all. Her responses to my following three letters were similar: friendly and pleasant but totally ignoring the subject I was most interested in.

I wrote my next letter in bold, indicating that it would be the last time I would mention my marriage proposal. Her response came much faster than her prior letters. She accepted my proposal, and I was thrilled! But I could not see us getting married in the immediate future. I needed an education and a good job first. I figured that we would probably marry after a four-year engagement, which meant that I would be 30 years old before we could get married.

Concentrated Counsel

In 1989, a few months after my 27th birthday, I read a talk that President Ezra Taft Benson had given the previous year in the priesthood session of general conference. The talk was titled "To the Single Adult Brethren of the Church." President Benson said: "To you single adult brethren, I want you to know of my great love for each of you. I have great expectations for you and a great hope in you. . . . You may be twenty-seven years of age, or thirty, or possibly even older."

With this mention of 27-year-old men, President Benson had my attention! Then he asked, "Just what are your priorities at this time in your life?" He suggested several priorities—prayer, study of the Book of Mormon and other scriptures, Church activity, dress and grooming, family relationships, moral cleanliness, temple marriage, academic and vocational goals, sharing the gospel, and community service.

For the rest of the talk, the prophet focused on one of these priorities: temple marriage. He quoted a letter he had received from a devoted mother and father who were concerned about their children delaying marriage because of education and other concerns. I continued reading, but I began losing interest. I reasoned that this message did not apply to young people in Africa, where we were poor and where jobs were very difficult to find.

Toward the end of the talk, President Benson said: "I realize that some of you brethren may have genuine fears regarding the real responsibilities that will be yours if you do marry. You are concerned about being able to support a wife and family and provide them with the necessities in these uncertain economic times. Those fears must be replaced with faith."[19] Even after reading this, I convinced myself that President Benson's message did not apply to me.

A full-time missionary serving in our area noticed the talk as well, and he decided it was his job to encourage me to follow President Benson's counsel. He highlighted a few passages in the talk and left it in a place where I would find it. I thought he was teasing me, so I ignored it. But that young missionary did not give up. He asked me how I understood the 7th verse of Amos chapter 3: "Surely the Lord God will do nothing, but he revealeth his secret unto his servants the prophets."

The following Sunday after church, my branch president, John Newbold, invited me into his office. He said, "Eddie, my wife and I were talking about you the other day. We see you after church playing with children, but you do not seem to take interest in these beautiful young ladies. Do you realize that you are getting old?"

The Holy Ghost helped me understand more than what President Newbold said. I knew what I needed to do, and I felt joy in what I had learned. I walked out of President Newbold's office with an expanded vision of the Lord's design for Naume and me. I now had a determination to talk with her about possible marriage dates.

Following the Creator's Plan for Our Eternal Destiny

On December 9, 1989, a few months after my visit with President Newbold and three years after that dream on my mission, Naume and I were married civilly. We could not yet afford to travel to the Johannesburg South Africa Temple to be sealed, but we were so happy to be together. As we saved our money so we could go to the temple, I began to develop a firm conviction of something President Benson said in his talk:

"Honorable marriage is more important than wealth, position, and status. As husband and wife, you can achieve your life's goals together. As you sacrifice for each other and your children, the Lord will bless you, and your commitment to the Lord and your service in His kingdom will be enhanced."[20]

*Edward and Naume on the day of their civil marriage, December 9, 1989.
Left to right: Edward's parents, Clement and Rose Dube; Edward and Naume;
Naume's parents, Anna and Bauleni Salizani*

Two and a half years later, Naume and I were finally able to travel to South Africa. We were sealed for time and all eternity on May 15, 1992, and our daughter Rosemary was sealed to us. Nothing I had experienced could compare with the joy and comfort I felt that day.

After we were sealed, we stood outside the temple, looking at each other without saying a word. After a while, Naume said, "What are you thinking?"

"I am filled with indescribable joy," I said.

She replied, "I feel happy to know that it is not only us as husband and wife who are sealed together but also Rose and the children who will come after her."

We talked about the far-reaching effects of our decision—the influence on our immediate family, our grandchildren, and their children throughout eternity.

Our joy has deepened since that day. Naume and I have worked together to be disciples of Jesus Christ and to help our children learn of Him and His restored gospel. We have seen that the family truly is "central to the Creator's plan for the eternal destiny of His children."[21] Temple ordinances and covenants have expanded our vision and taught us of our divine origin and potential.

Was it a coincidence that the counsel from the Lord's prophet, the good-natured pressure from a missionary, and the visit with my branch president came together at that time? No. As President Thomas S. Monson taught, "The Lord is in the details of our lives."[22]

Looking back at those days, I am truly grateful for the Lord's servants—particularly a prophet and a branch president who worthily held keys and received inspiration to say the right things at the right time.

Because Naume and I followed their counsel, we have received the promise of eternal blessings. We will be together forever if we remain faithful, and our children will be ours throughout eternity. I cherish these indescribable blessings each day.

Edward, Naume, and Rosemary at the time of their sealing, 1992

This simple pattern repeats itself in the lives of Heavenly Father's children throughout the world. The Lord really is in the

Edward and Naume pondering outside the temple after their sealing, May 15, 1992

details of our lives. We just need to look to see Him there. His timely counsel often comes to us through His prophet, our local Church leaders, our family and friends, and the promptings of the Holy Ghost. And this timely counsel leads to timeless blessings—temple blessings, which outweigh any challenges and any earthly hopes.

Marriage between a man and a woman is ordained of God. . . . Sacred ordinances and covenants available in holy temples make it possible for individuals to return to the presence of God and for families to be united eternally.

"THE FAMILY: A PROCLAMATION TO THE WORLD"

CHAPTER 12

A Power Stronger Than Tradition

"True religion," taught Elder Dieter F. Uchtdorf, "should not originate from what pleases men or the traditions of ancestors, but rather from what pleases God, our Eternal Father."[23]

President Dallin H. Oaks taught of a gospel culture that is higher than cultural or family traditions. "This gospel culture," he said, "comes from the plan of salvation, the commandments of God, and the teachings of the living prophets. It guides us in the way we raise our families and live our individual lives. . . . To help its members all over the world, the Church teaches us to give up any personal or family traditions or practices that are contrary to the teachings of the Church of Jesus Christ and to this gospel culture."[24]

When Naume and I were brand-new parents, we experienced the tension between the traditions of our ancestors and the gospel of Jesus Christ.

A Necklace and a Warning

We were excited for my mother to visit us and our firstborn child, her new granddaughter, Rosemary. We were eager to learn everything my mother would teach us about raising a child.

Upon arriving at our home, Mother reached into her bag and brought out a necklace. The necklace appeared to be nothing but a circle of knitted cloth. But within that cloth was a series of beads made of plants, with a fiber string running through them. The cloth protected the necklace, which, my mother explained,

was an amulet—a magical object. She held out the cloth-encircled necklace and instructed Naume to put it on Rosemary's neck.

Sensing Naume's hesitation, Mother immediately said, "From an early age my mother and maternal grandmother gave me this magical object, which has protected me and all my children, including your husband. This amulet will protect your daughter from diseases and from all sorts of spells that might befall her, and she will overcome any difficult situation in life. She will need to wear this until she is five years old."

Four generations, 1990: Naume washing clothes with her sister Tandiwe; Naume's mother, Anna (standing in back); and Naume's grandmother Keresia Mhako Zuari (in front), holding Rosemary

Throughout my life, my mother had taught me to trust the Lord, but sometimes even she failed to look to Him, allowing cultural traditions to obscure her faith. Naume and I were members of the restored Church of Jesus Christ, and we were determined to abandon cultural traditions that were not consistent with gospel truths.

We turned to my mother and explained that because I was serving as branch president in our local congregation, I would not be comfortable placing the necklace on our child. My mother replied with a warning: without the necklace, our baby would die.

A Prompting and a Blessing

A few weeks after this incident, our little Rosemary became very ill, and we did not have money to take her to the doctor. Late at night, I started thinking about my mother's warning. In my panic, I wished I had accepted the necklace and put it on Rosemary's neck.

For just a moment, I was like the Pharisees, whom the Lord reproved for their false traditions. He said, "In vain do they worship me, teaching for doctrines the commandments of men. For laying aside the commandment of God, ye hold the tradition of men. . . . Full well ye reject the commandment of God, that ye may keep your own tradition" (Mark 7:7–9).

The next moment, I heard a still, small voice urging me to exercise faith in the Lord Jesus Christ, counseling me to guard against any traditions that might limit our family's progress on the covenant path, reminding me of what God saw in me as a priesthood holder. I immediately dressed in my Sunday best. I took our baby in my arms and gave her a priesthood blessing. I felt peace and comfort, and I sensed that Naume felt the same way. Almost immediately, both Naume and little Rosemary fell into a peaceful sleep.

Our daughter Rosemary was healed. In the following days,

she slowly recovered and regained her full health. What a miracle we witnessed when we looked to the Lord and exercised faith in Him! In His tender mercy, He reached out to us and blessed our daughter, with a power stronger than any cultural tradition.

I think of Peter's words to the Saints in his day. He spoke of some people who "stumble at the word" of the Lord (1 Peter 2:8). Such people stumble because they refuse to let go of traditions. "But ye are a chosen generation," Peter declared, "a royal priesthood, an holy nation, a peculiar people; that ye should shew forth the praises of him who hath called you out of darkness into his marvellous light" (1 Peter 2:9). Our most meaningful traditions should lead us to keep the Lord's commandments and honor sacred covenants. I think of joyful traditions such as keeping the Sabbath day holy, participating in family home evening, and going to the temple with children to perform baptisms for the dead. Such traditions guide us toward our eternal potential—away from the darkness of the world, rejoicing in the Lord's marvelous light.

Look unto me in every thought; doubt not, fear not.

DOCTRINE AND COVENANTS 6:36

CHAPTER 13

Pressing toward the Mark

The Apostle Paul said: "This one thing I do, forgetting those things which are behind, and reaching forth unto those things which are before, I press toward the mark for the prize of the high calling of God in Christ Jesus" (Philippians 3:13–14).

Paul is not the only gospel teacher who has shared this vision of our potential. I also learned it from my mother.

"Look Ahead"

In the introduction to this book, I tell the story of my mother teaching me to work in our field. "Never look back," she said. "Look ahead at what we still have to do!"

This lesson has remained with me ever since the day Mother shared it. Whether she knew it or not, she was preparing me to do more than work diligently in our field. She was preparing me to embrace the restored gospel of Jesus Christ and serve in His Church. She was preparing me to make and keep sacred covenants. Like Paul, she was "reaching forth unto those things which are before." Throughout her life, she would continue teaching me to reach forth and to "press toward the mark."

"Our Home Is in Heaven"

When I was seven years old, my maternal grandmother died. I loved her so much, and I was heartbroken when she was no longer in our home. I was especially sad in the mornings when I sat in our kitchen. I remembered the times when Grandmother cooked porridge with peanut butter for me before I went to school.

One of those mornings, my mother recognized my sense of loss. She felt devastated herself—the death of her dear mother was more heartbreaking for her than it was for anyone else. But even in her sorrow, she seized the opportunity to teach me an important lesson. She stopped what she was doing, sat next to me, looked into my eyes, and said, "This is not our home. Our home is in heaven!"

My mother's words comforted me and inspired my young and tender heart. They would comfort and inspire me about 28 years later, when I watched helplessly as she suffered from cancer.

"It Is Up to God"

For much of the time Mother battled cancer, she lived with my family and me. One night I heard her sobbing in her bedroom. Her pain was intense, even after taking her last daily dose of morphine only two hours earlier.

I entered her room and sobbed with her. I prayed aloud for her to receive instant relief from her pain. And then she did the same thing she had done in the field and in the kitchen: she stopped and taught me a lesson. I will never forget her face at that moment: frail, stricken, and full of pain, gazing with pity on her sorrowing son. She smiled through her tears, looked directly into my eyes, and said, "It is not up to you or anyone else, but it is up to God whether this pain will go away or not."

I sat up quietly. She too sat quietly. The scene remains vivid in my mind. That night, through my mother, the Lord taught me a lesson that will stay with me forever. As my mother expressed her acceptance of God's will, I remembered the reason Jesus Christ suffered in the Garden of Gethsemane and on Golgotha. He said: "Behold I have given unto you my gospel, and this is the gospel which I have given unto you—that I came into the world to do the will of my Father, because my Father sent me" (3 Nephi 27:13).

My mother, even in her severe pain, reached out to me, showed me how to accept God's will, and helped me prepare to serve in the Lord's kingdom, under any circumstance. My testimony grew stronger as I came to understand more deeply my loving Savior's experience with the bitter cup that terrible night in Gethsemane and, later, on the cross. His plaintive plea and His submission to His Father established our way to salvation and set the example for us to follow: "Father, if thou be willing, remove this cup from me: nevertheless not my will, but thine, be done" (Luke 22:42).

Blessed by My Mother's Influence

I was not the only one blessed by my mother's influence in the final days of her life. On October 2, 1997, Mother was admitted to Parirenyatwa Hospital in Harare, Zimbabwe. I watched her smile bravely and utter uplifting words to people who visited her. The nurses said she was a delight to serve because of her positive attitude. She always asked visitors to pray by her hospital bed. Even though she was frail and consumed with pain and grief, she continued to find opportunities to teach and testify of the Lord Jesus Christ.

My brother Clement was visiting Mother in the hospital

one day when he told her that he had to leave for an important business meeting. He had a prestigious job with a large retail food chain in Zimbabwe. She stopped him with this question: "Clement, are you still planning to be a pastor?" Seeing his hesitation, she reminded him that from the time he was very young, he had always wanted to be a pastor. She urged him not to let worldly things take that desire away from him. She then recited Matthew 6:33 from memory: "Seek ye first the kingdom of God, and his righteousness; and all these things shall be added unto you."

Following Mother's deathbed counsel, Clement gave up his job and commenced an intensive course of training to become a pastor in the Methodist Church of Zimbabwe—the church she had joined late in her life. He later earned a PhD in New Testament studies and served as dean of the United Theological Institute of Zimbabwe.

Letting Mother Go

On the evening of October 10, 1997, I offered a prayer by my mother's bedside, along with Naume, Clement, and Clement's wife, Lillian. For the first time since Mother began her battle with cancer, I asked Heavenly Father to let her pass from this life if it was His will. I immediately felt peace. I knew that Mother was going to die that night, but I did not tell anyone. This was a sacred experience for me. The Savior's words to His Apostles, just before His death, sank deep in my soul: "Let not your heart be troubled: ye believe in God, believe also in me. In my Father's house are many mansions: if it were not so, I would have told you. I go to prepare a place for you" (John 14:1–2).

The next morning when we went to the hospital, one of the nurses met us and confirmed what I had known since the night before: Mother had passed away.

At this time, my only sister, Theresa, was also in the hospital. She was suffering from a complication connected with the birth of her daughter Vimbai six months earlier. Theresa died a week after Mother passed away, leaving her husband, Luckymore Pindeni, and three children—Vimbai, John, and Constance—without a wife and mother in their home.

If it were not for my mother's lessons, these two losses would have been devastating for me. Because I believed what she had taught me about looking ahead to our home in heaven and accepting God's will, I was at peace even though I was deeply saddened. Her teachings, combined with my understanding of the eternal nature of the family, comforted me.

At the end of her life, my mother followed the example of our Master, our Savior Jesus Christ, who looked up to His Father in every way—even when His suffering was unrelenting, even when His anguish increased, with more pressure, more torture, and more agony. In His intercessory prayer, He proclaimed, "I have glorified thee on the earth: I have finished the work which thou gavest me to do" (John 17:4). On the cross, He cried out "with a loud voice, saying, Father, it is finished, thy will is done" (Joseph Smith Translation, Matthew 27:54).

Keeping Mother Close

Solomon declared: "Where there is no vision, the people perish: but he that keepeth the law, happy is he" (Proverbs 29:18). Paul's declaration about "reaching forth" and "press[ing] toward the mark" gives us a vision of our home in heaven (Philippians 3:13–14). My mother's teachings have soothed me, lifted me, inspired me, and helped me see beyond my surroundings—beyond the mango tree, beyond the field, beyond the village, beyond a hospital room.

"Never look back. Look ahead."

"This is not our home. Our home is in heaven."

"It is not up to you or anyone else, but it is up to God."

As Mother worked by our sides, she did not look back at the work behind us. And she saw more than the physical work ahead of us. She knew that we are "strangers and pilgrims on the earth," and she "desire[d] a better country, that is, an heavenly" (Hebrews 11:13, 16). She instilled that same desire in us.

Today she does not work by our sides as she did before, but my prayer is that we will keep her close and that her legacy of faith will live on for generations to come.

> Ye must press forward with a steadfastness in Christ,
> having a perfect brightness of hope, and a love of God
> and of all men. Wherefore, if ye shall press forward,
> feasting upon the word of Christ, and endure to the end,
> behold, thus saith the Father: Ye shall have eternal life.
>
> 2 NEPHI 31:20

CHAPTER 14

Faith to Go,
Faith to Stay

From *Lectures on Faith*, we learn that faith "is the moving cause of all action."[25] Sometimes the action of faith means that we *go*—like Nephi, who declared: "I will go and do the things which the Lord hath commanded, for I know that the Lord giveth no commandments unto the children of men, save he shall prepare a way for them that they may accomplish the thing which he commandeth them" (1 Nephi 3:7).

Sometimes the action of faith means that we *stay*—like Nehemiah, who resisted people's attempts to distract him from rebuilding the wall around Jerusalem. "I am doing a great work," Nehemiah said, "so that I cannot come down: why should the work cease, whilst I leave it, and come down to you?" (Nehemiah 6:3).

My dear wife, Naume, is a great strength to me. Over the years, she has taught me to turn to the Lord in all things. I have seen her exercise the faith to go and the faith to stay.

Naume's Conversion

Naume Keresia Salizani was born in Bindura, Mashonaland Central, Zimbabwe, the third of nine children. Her parents are Bauleni Salizani, from Malawi, and Anna Mhako Salizani, from Zimbabwe. Bauleni and Anna raised their children in Zimbabwe in the Apostolic Faith Mission Church, teaching them from the Bible and helping them exercise faith in Jesus Christ. Naume enjoyed going to church with her family.

Edward with members of the Salizani family, about 1990. Left to right: Edward, Naume, Omega, Maybe, and Andrew

When Naume was 14 years old, her brother Lazarus joined The Church of Jesus Christ of Latter-day Saints. A year later, Naume and her brother Amos began meeting with the missionaries. As one of those missionaries, I witnessed Naume's conversion.

While Naume participated in the missionary lessons, she began attending the local branch of the Church. Her first Sunday there was a life-changing experience. She was impressed with the talks in sacrament meeting and the classes she attended. She made friends right away. She felt the influence of the Spirit as she learned about the Book of Mormon and the Prophet Joseph Smith.

My companion and I finished teaching Naume the lessons,

and her brother Lazarus baptized her just before he departed on his own mission.

After Naume was baptized, she never missed church on Sunday. She enjoyed Young Women activities and enrolled in seminary. The Church became the most important thing in her life. All her activities and associations were Church related. She made a commitment to love and respect the Lord, and she was determined that she would marry someone who demonstrated love and respect

Naume and Edward Dube in front of the Salt Lake Temple, 1995

for Him. I feel honored and privileged that several years later, she agreed to marry me.

Throughout her life, Naume has turned to the Lord in all things. Examples of her faith are too numerous to recount. I will share two of them.

Faith to Go to Church

Shortly after we were married, I was called to preside over a group in Mbizo Township, which subsequently became a branch. We lived in Newtown, which was about 15 kilometers (9.3 miles) from the Mbizo meetinghouse.

Naume and I did not always have money for transportation to and from Mbizo, so we walked to church and back home almost every Sunday. Even when Naume was expecting our first child, Rosemary, she made the long walk to church. She was serving as Primary president at the time. After our meetings, she sat and waited patiently under a mango tree while I interviewed members of the branch. Then we walked home together.

She was a great blessing to the members of our little branch, who were inspired by her service and by our teamwork as husband and wife. This little branch produced missionaries who continued serving the Church as leaders in Zimbabwe.

I'm grateful that Naume had faith to *go*.

Faith to Stay and Serve

In 1997, I had a good job. I was a country director in the Church Educational System, overseeing the work in Malawi, Zambia, and Zimbabwe. I was serving in the Church as president of the Harare Zimbabwe District. Naume and I were renting a home in Harare, but we wanted a home of our own, so we bought

land in Norton, which was about a 40-minute drive from the big city. For the next two years, I often drove to Norton early in the morning to deliver bags of cement or other supplies and to carefully monitor the construction project. By 1999, we had built a three-bedroom house. Our plan was to move there and to build a bigger home—our dream home—on the property.

Edward painting the house in Norton, 2000

President Frank Bagley, the mission president and my ecclesiastical leader, was disappointed when we told him about our plan. He counseled us not to move to Norton, which would be outside the stake boundaries when the district became a stake. We responded that if we continued to rent a home in Harare, we would not be able to build our larger home in Norton. President Bagley shared this information with Elder Christoffel Golden Jr., who was serving as an Area Seventy at the time and who was also my immediate supervisor in the Church Educational System. Elder Golden concurred with President Bagley. He suggested that we stay in Harare and prepare our new home in Norton as rental property. Again we resisted this counsel. We could not charge as much for the Norton property as we were paying in Harare. We would lose money and never be able to build our dream home.

Soon after these conversations, Elder Dennis E. Simmons, a General Authority, visited the area. President and Sister Bagley invited Naume and me to the mission home to eat dinner with them and Elder and Sister Simmons. The subject of our Norton home came up in the conversation, and Elder Simmons gave us the same counsel we had heard from President Bagley and Elder Golden. He said that I would be able to watch over the Church more effectively if we stayed in Harare. I countered that a move to Norton would be better for our family.

On the way home that night, Naume asked me why I was being so stubborn. I responded that our leaders did not seem to understand our situation. She said that she would support me only if I was willing to follow our Church leaders' counsel. Needless to say, we remained in Harare.

We never built our dream home, but we were richly blessed.

We continued serving in the Church, and I was called to be the president of the Harare Zimbabwe Stake on December 12, 1999.

First stake presidency in Zimbabwe, December 12, 1999.
Left to right: Leonard S. Chisango, Edward Dube, and Charles Maphosa

As Naume and I served the members of our stake, we grew closer to each other. Our extraordinary children—Rosemary, Rachel, Edward Jr., and Edith—also had wonderful experiences in the city. They developed the confidence and outgoing natures they would need later, when we moved to the United States.

At first, I didn't realize that my Church leaders were expressing the will of the Lord when they advised us to stay in Harare. The Lord, who saw the big picture, knew that we needed to be in Harare so we could serve in the stake and so we could become the people He wanted us to become.

I'm grateful that Naume had faith to *stay.*

Aligning with the Lord's Will

Our quest should always be to learn the Lord's will and align ourselves with it. As I reflect on my struggles to do this, I see that my problem has always been pride. Either I have been too concerned about temporal things or I have lacked the humility to see myself as the Lord has wanted me to be. I have often worried too much about what I want to receive and not enough about what I can give as an instrument in the Lord's hands. As a result, I have sometimes been too slow to go where He wants me to go and too stubborn to stay when He wants me to stay.

As we align ourselves with the Lord's will, we find that our life gains more meaning. Our motivations change. Rather than seeking compensation, we seek opportunities to make a difference in the lives of people in our family, at church, at work, and in the community. The rewards we desire also change. Rather than looking for personal acclaim, we hope for the satisfaction and joy of knowing that our time in this mortal life is well spent—that through us, the Lord is blessing others.

The Dube children in 2010.
Left to right: Rosemary, Rachel, Edward Jr., Edith

If the veil were opened to us and we could see eternity, we would all rally behind the Lord and follow His example. We would find it easier to work with energy and passion to make a difference in the world. But an open veil would defeat the purpose of why we are here. It would remove the need to "walk by faith, not by sight" (2 Corinthians 5:7).

As it is, we have the privilege of learning to receive and follow the Lord's voice. Sometimes He commands us—as He commanded the Israelites who were trapped between the Red Sea and Pharaoh's pursuing army—to "fear ye not, stand still." Soon after that, he might command us—as He commanded them—to "go forward" immediately. If we have faith to go and faith to stay, we will, like the Israelites, "see the salvation of the Lord" in our lives and in the lives of those we love (Exodus 14:13–15).

> I do not know all things; but the Lord knoweth
> all things which are to come; wherefore, he
> worketh in me to do according to his will.
>
> WORDS OF MORMON 1:7

CHAPTER 15

In the Hands of God

In January 2000, a few weeks after I was called to serve as president of the Harare Zimbabwe Stake, Elder Jeffrey R. Holland of the Quorum of the Twelve Apostles visited Zimbabwe to minister to the Latter-day Saints there. As part of his assignment, he met with our new stake presidency, the high council, and the bishops in the stake. For a couple of hours, we sat in a semicircle and learned from an Apostle of Jesus Christ about leadership in the Lord's restored Church.

At one point in our training session, Elder Holland warned us of three things that destroy leaders in The Church of Jesus Christ of Latter-day Saints: financial dishonesty, immorality, and the teaching of false doctrine. Then he directed his words to me. He walked to the place where I was sitting, knelt in front of me, and said, "President, I beg you, study the scriptures and handbooks every day."

That apostolic plea touched my soul profoundly and personally. But Elder Holland was not speaking only to me, Edward Dube. He was speaking to President Edward Dube, a servant-leader of a flock of Saints. Five years later, those Saints would need me to have an abiding testimony of what Elder Holland said—and they would need to strengthen that testimony within themselves.

Homeless but Not Hopeless

In 2005, the Zimbabwe government began what they called Operation Murambatsvina, meaning "move the rubbish"—also called Operation Restore Order. Police destroyed, on a massive scale, alleged illegal structures where people lived with their extended families. Through this action, at least 700,000 people lost their homes and jobs. About 2.4 million people were affected indirectly.[26] Some people were able to salvage a few possessions, but most had nowhere to go. Tens of thousands of Zimbabweans were left homeless during the rainy winter season.

At least half of the members of our stake, especially those who lived in the high-density housing areas, were directly affected by Operation Murambatsvina. Many of them moved to rural areas and cities where the Church was not organized; others left the country. Before the government operation, average sacrament meeting attendance in one ward in the stake was approximately 300. We thought it might be time to divide it into two wards. Following Operation Murambatsvina, average sacrament meeting attendance in that ward dropped to 110.

What can a leader say to a large group of people who have lost almost all their material possessions and who fear for their families' lives? Remembering Elder Holland's counsel, I felt inspired to urge them to carry on as though nothing was wrong. I encouraged them to continue with daily scripture study and prayer and weekly family home evening.

As the economic and political challenges persisted, I knelt and pled with Heavenly Father to know whether I had told the members the right thing. He blessed me with a clear, peaceful assurance. That assurance deepened when I saw members of our stake who stayed true to the faith even during severe trials.

I remember returning from a training trip to South Africa during this period. When Naume met me at the airport, she said she wasn't going to take me home immediately. We needed to go to Mbare township to visit the family of a sister who had just died. As we drove through the community, we saw demolished homes everywhere. We saw a mother cooking a meal outside, using her furniture as firewood.

We met with Church members in the area. As we sat outside singing hymns, we noticed that our little group was growing. Neighbors who were not members of the Church heard our singing and joined us for comfort. We shared testimonies of the Lord Jesus Christ and His Atonement. We cried together for our sister who had died and for others among us who suffered.

A few months later, during the June 2005 stake conference, I observed hundreds in the congregation who hadn't been able to bathe for weeks and had lost nearly everything. As we sang together "Come, Come, Ye Saints," I couldn't hold back my tears. Their faith inspired me. Some of them slept under bridges because they were now homeless, but they still chose to come to stake conference and worship with us. They had lost shelter but had not lost hope. Their faith deepened as they experienced these trials.

As I marveled at the faith of my brothers and sisters in the stake, I was reminded of the prophet Mormon, who also stayed true during a time of terrible adversity. He said: "Know ye not that ye are in the hands of God? Know ye not that he hath all power, and at his great command the earth shall be rolled together as a scroll?" (Mormon 5:23). He wrote those words as a warning to the wicked, but I thought the faithful members of our stake would see them as words of encouragement. I could imagine them answering Mormon's questions: "Yes, we know we are in the hands of God, and we know that He has all power. That is precisely why we have hope, even when everything seems hopeless."

Those persevering Saints reminded me of something else Mormon said: "What is it that ye shall hope for? Behold I say unto you that ye shall have hope through the atonement of Christ and the power of his resurrection, to be raised unto life eternal, and this because of your faith in him according to his promise" (Moroni 7:41). When we have this hope, the Lord can lift us above any hardship or sorrow.

Ministering One by One

Early in 2005, before these tragic events occurred, my counselors and I were planning to submit a recommendation to divide the stake into three new stakes. Now we talked about combining wards and branches and even closing some of them. However, I felt this wasn't a good idea. Together we decided to strive to re-build each ward and branch. This gave members of the stake an opportunity to minister one by one.

My counselors and I worked closely with the high council to review key indicators of growth and strength in the Church. Following the guidance of the handbook, as Elder Holland had advised, we assigned high councilors to serve on committees. For example, some high councilors worked closely with ward Relief Societies, elders quorums, and high priest groups. Others worked with a committee that focused on Aaronic Priesthood quorums and Young Women classes. This gave the stake presidency more time to reach out to individual members. We also regularly inter-viewed priesthood leaders in the stake. We received an accounting of their work, and we helped them set goals and make plans to accomplish them.

All the leaders in the stake—including the stake presidency, bishoprics, Relief Society presidencies, high priests group leaderships, elders quorum presidencies, and Aaronic Priesthood and Young Women leaders—focused on individual members. Each leader accepted accountability and asked the same of the members of his or her organization. Can you imagine what happened? Average sacrament meeting attendance went up, as did other key indicators of growth and strength. Missionary efforts increased and improved. Individual members were strengthened in their faith in the Lord Jesus Christ. We saw the wisdom in something President Thomas S. Monson had taught: "When performance is measured, performance improves. When performance is measured and reported, the rate of improvement accelerates."[27]

The leaders in our stake raised individual Saints' expectations and helped them see beyond their present problems. Zimbabwe's severe economic and political upheavals were swallowed up in our efforts to love and strengthen one another. We humbled ourselves and worked together with a common goal: to invite others to come unto Christ. As we relied on the Lord more and more, He blessed us with greater energy, boosted our creativity, and expanded our vision so we could see a little bit more of what He saw in us and those around us. We felt the power and reality of something President Russell M. Nelson, then a member of the Quorum of the Twelve Apostles, taught that same year in general conference: "When sore trials come upon us, it's time to deepen our faith in God, to work hard, and to serve others. Then He will heal our broken hearts. He will bestow upon us personal peace and comfort. Those great gifts will not be destroyed, even by death."[28]

*The Dube family with Elder Christoffel Golden Jr.
and Elder Russell M. Nelson at the
Harare Zimbabwe Stake Conference, 2004*

By June 2008, after years of political turmoil and economic meltdown, inflation in Zimbabwe had grown to 231 million percent. The Zimbabwean dollar was worthless. But our stake emerged with spiritual and temporal strength. We also emerged with a new stake of Zion in Harare, created in the midst of affliction. Eight years later, two additional stakes were created in Harare. The Lord had fulfilled His promise among His people in our stake: "Behold, I will go before you and be your rearward; and I will be in your midst, and you shall not be confounded" (Doctrine and Covenants 49:27).

The Lord extends this promise of peace to all of us, even as we experience personal trials and even as we mourn because of pain and suffering and injustice throughout the world. Even when things are wrong all around us, we can keep things right in our personal lives. The Lord will not forget us. We are in His hands, and He is ready to help us if we are ready to receive His help.

In the world ye shall have tribulation: but be of
good cheer; I have overcome the world.

JOHN 16:33

CHAPTER 16

Hearts Pricked

When I was serving as a stake president, Naume and I were invited to the office of our bishop, Albert Mutariswa, for tithing settlement. After we declared that we were full-tithe payers, Bishop Mutariswa asked us a question that surprised us. He said, "Why have you opted to pay all your tithing at the end of the year even though you receive your income monthly?"

Naume and I looked at each other and then looked at Bishop Mutariswa. We explained that it was convenient for us to pay tithing at the end of the year.

In response, Bishop Mutariswa mentioned Abel's offering of "the firstlings of his flock and of the fat thereof" (Genesis 4:4; see also Moses 5:20). He said that Abel's choice to offer the firstlings, to contribute the very best, showed his love for God. Our bishop then said: "I like to give my 10 percent to the Lord as my very first payment when I receive my income. The Lord has given me all that I possess. I therefore pay my tithing each month with great joy for what He has given me."

Naume and I left the bishop's office dumbfounded. Just

four years before that conversation, I had interviewed Albert Mutariswa, a recent convert, as he prepared to receive the Melchizedek Priesthood. Now this man had the courage to suggest that I, his stake president, change the way I paid tithing. I was astonished and inspired, and Naume and I resolved that we would pay our tithing first, before anything else.

Before I say more, I hasten to point out that the frequency of tithe paying is an individual decision, between each person or couple and the Lord. For some, it may be best to pay tithing once, at the end of the year. However, Naume and I have found Bishop Mutariswa's counsel to be very helpful for us.

Grateful for a Courageous Bishop

The Lord has blessed us immensely, beyond our comprehension, as we have paid tithing—especially as we have adopted Bishop Mutariswa's pattern. For us, paying tithing at the end of the year was like sitting under the shade of the mango tree. It was comfortable and convenient, and it was good. We are grateful that our courageous bishop encouraged us to move beyond that shade and do something that, in our circumstances, was even better.

One blessing we have received is that we have learned to be more responsible with our money, to plan and budget efficiently. Even greater are the spiritual blessings the Lord has given us. As Elder David A. Bednar has taught: "Windows allow natural light to enter into a building. In like manner, spiritual illumination and perspective are poured out through the windows of heaven and into our lives as we honor the law of tithing."[29]

We will forever be grateful for a thoughtful and inspired bishop, who "did prick [our] hearts with the word" (Jarom 1:12). His courage to speak gave us courage to change, and that change has helped us walk the covenant path as we strive to return to the Lord.

"Return unto me," the Lord says, "and I will return unto you. . . . But ye said, Wherein shall we return? Will a man rob God? Yet ye have robbed me. But ye say, Wherein have we robbed thee? In tithes and offerings" (Malachi 3:7–8; see also 3 Nephi 24:7–8).

Did Naume and I rob God when we waited until the end of the year to offer our tithing? No. But we learned that in our situation, we could give that offering more readily and faithfully if we would give it as soon as we received income.

"Bring ye all the tithes into the storehouse, . . . and prove me now herewith, saith the Lord of hosts, if I will not open you the windows of heaven, and pour you out a blessing, that there shall not be room enough to receive it" (Malachi 3:10; see also 3 Nephi 24:10).

Leading with the Heart, for the Heart

When Bishop Mutariswa shared this counsel with us, he followed a pattern that President Russell M. Nelson had taught a few years earlier. President Nelson said that each Church leader "has been called to face the people as a representative of the Lord, not the other way around."[30] He has given the following counsel to leaders:

"Teach with a two-pronged approach:

- "Bear pure testimony of Jesus Christ and His doctrine, and
- "Issue a bold invitation to take righteous action. . . .

"When a leader bears pure testimony of Jesus Christ and the divinity of His doctrine, the Holy Ghost bears witness of its truth. When this witness is offered with the pure love of Jesus Christ, those who choose to hear will feel the Lord's love for them. And if they open their hearts to the Savior, they will begin to be 'illuminated by the light of the everlasting word' (Alma 5:7)."[31]

This approach has a great effect because it goes to the heart. When leaders bear testimony of the Savior and His doctrine and extend invitations to act, they help others prepare for the Lord to "put [His] law in their inward parts, and write it in their hearts" (Jeremiah 31:33).

Listening with a Desire to Act

Several years after Naume and I received Bishop Mutariswa's wise advice, I met a good sister who was not giving enough attention to her bishop's counsel. I was attending a ward as a visiting authority, and a woman in the ward pulled me out of a priesthood meeting. With tears in her eyes, she said, "Elder Dube, I am sad and confused. Will you please help me? My husband and I are separated, and we are strongly contemplating a divorce. I went to my bishop for counsel and he told me one thing, and then I went to my stake president and he told me something different."

I smiled and asked, "Dear sister, are you shopping for ideas?"

She paused and cried a little more and said, "No, I need some help."

I didn't ask this sister to tell me the whole story—that is the bishop's role. I didn't ask her to repeat the counsel she had received from each leader—that was not for me to know. I was certain that her bishop was called of God and that he could receive inspiration to guide members of his ward, so I asked, "Do you promise to follow my counsel?"

She said yes, apparently anticipating that I would share new words of wisdom.

I said, "Go again to your bishop. As you talk with him and

as he shares counsel with you, listen with a desire to act upon the impressions you receive. Then act on those impressions."

She agreed to do so. I later learned that she followed through with her commitment. She and her husband were able to resolve their differences, and now they are happily married.

I am grateful for bishops and other leaders who are "called of God, by prophecy, and by the laying on of hands by those who are in authority" (Articles of Faith 1:5). We are blessed, as families and individuals, when we follow their counsel.

> And now I would that ye should be humble, and be submissive and gentle; easy to be entreated; full of patience and long-suffering; being temperate in all things; being diligent in keeping the commandments of God at all times; asking for whatsoever things ye stand in need, both spiritual and temporal; always returning thanks unto God for whatsoever things ye do receive.
>
> ALMA 7:23

CHAPTER 17

Look Up to the Lord

On June 26, 2009, Elder Russell M. Nelson of the Quorum of the Twelve Apostles welcomed Naume and me into his office in Salt Lake City, Utah. We were about to be set apart to work together as mission companions in the Zimbabwe Harare Mission for the next three years. During that time, I would serve as mission president.

At one point in our conversation, Elder Nelson looked directly into my eyes and said, "President, with those missionaries"—I leaned forward, anxious to hear every word from this Apostle—"help them to look up to the Lord!" Elder Nelson emphasized this counsel by pointing up to heaven.

A New Initiative

What did it mean for missionaries to look up to the Lord? And how could I—a young man from rural Zimbabwe—help them do it? As I began my service as a mission president, I felt my inadequacy. I asked myself, "Who am I to inspire these young people, from diverse cultures and experience, to exercise faith and look up to the Lord?"

I considered using impressive, professional-looking materials that missionaries could display on the walls of their apartments. Such things, used at the right time and in the right place, can be motivating and effective. But the more I pondered my responsibility at that time and in that place, the more I remembered the simplicity of

Naume and Edward in Nauvoo, Illinois, en route to the meeting with Elder Nelson and the new mission presidents' seminar in 2009

Elder Nelson's words: "Help them to look up to the Lord!" Those words stirred me up. They rang vividly in my mind and sank deeply into my heart.

As I counseled with Naume and with my assistants about what Elder Nelson had said, I realized that one way to look up to the Lord is to strive to become like Him. My assistants and I were drawn to *Preach My Gospel*, chapter 6, titled "How Do I Develop Christlike Attributes?" We also focused on the resurrected Savior's words to His disciples in the Americas: "What manner of men [and women] ought ye to be? Verily I say unto you, even as I am" (3 Nephi 27:27). We developed a simple initiative called "The Challenge to Become."

In this initiative, we identified five attributes from chapter 6 of *Preach My Gospel:* faith, obedience, charity and love, knowledge, and diligence. We asked each missionary to make the following commitments:

- Each morning I will take five minutes to choose an attribute I will work on throughout the day.
- Each day during my labor I will take five minutes to review my chosen attribute and evaluate how I am doing.
- Each night before I retire to bed, I will take five minutes to review my chosen attribute and ask Heavenly Father for strength and courage to become like my Savior, Jesus Christ, by seeking to incorporate His attributes into my life.
- In my planning session each day, I will review with my companion the progress I am making and ask him or her to help me improve on these Christlike attributes.
- I will remember that only through the power of Jesus Christ and His Atonement can I achieve this goal and help others.

The Dube family, 2009. Left to right: Naume, Edith, Rosemary, Rachel, Edward Jr., and Edward

Living Well and Serving Well

As we embraced this initiative, we were inspired, as a mission and as individuals, not only to be obedient and diligent but to seek the Lord's help in overcoming every growth-restricting obstacle in our path. Our purpose as missionaries—to "invite others to come unto Christ by helping them receive the restored gospel through faith in Jesus Christ and His Atonement, repentance, baptism, receiving the gift of the Holy Ghost, and enduring to the end"[32]—became our focus. All other things fell off and became irrelevant. We became more effective in doing the Lord's work, and our lives and relationships with each other improved. As we followed Elder Nelson's counsel to look up to the Lord, we learned the truth of something he had said a few years earlier:

"Many individuals don't know where to find God, and exclude Him from their lives. When spiritual needs arise, they may look to the left, the right, or round about. But looking to other people on the same level cannot satisfy spiritual shortages. . . .

"Trees reach up for the light and grow in the process. So do we as sons and daughters of heavenly parents. Facing upward provides a loftier perspective than facing right or facing left. Looking up in search of holiness builds strength and dignity as disciples of Deity. . . .

"In rendering service to others, which way do we face? From the right or the left, we can only push or pull. We can lift only from a higher plane. To reach it we don't look sideways; we look up to our Master. Just as we must look to God to *live* well, so we must look to God to *serve* well."[33]

We experienced sweet tranquility in the knowledge that we had helped others come unto Christ. We learned a principle that can guide all disciples of the Savior—that as we look up to Him, others can feel inspired to do the same.

Now, years later, Naume and I are overjoyed to see what these missionaries and their spouses have become. They have

Elder and Sister Dube at a reunion of missionaries from the
Zimbabwe Harare Mission, April 1, 2016

remembered to look up to the Lord. As they have looked up to Him, He has expanded their vision and helped them see themselves as He sees them. They are sharing this vision with their children, who, in time, will share it with their children.

> Come unto Christ, and be perfected in him, and
> deny yourselves of all ungodliness; and if ye shall deny
> yourselves of all ungodliness, and love God with all your
> might, mind and strength, then is his grace sufficient for
> you, that by his grace ye may be perfect in Christ.
>
> MORONI 10:32

CHAPTER 18

What the Lord Sees in Us

Naume looked at me with surprise when I told her about the email I had received. It was from the office of President Dieter F. Uchtdorf of the First Presidency, requesting a video conference with him in a few days.

Naume was serving at the time as stake young women president, and I was serving as an Area Seventy in Harare. We had also worked side by side for three years when I presided over the Zimbabwe Harare Mission. We expected to continue serving throughout our lives, but we never expected a special appointment with a member of the First Presidency. What was the purpose of this meeting? We couldn't imagine. We waited—anxious, nervous, expectant, excited.

When the day of our video conference arrived—January 17, 2013—we went early to my office, where I worked for the Church Educational System. For two hours, we paced around the building, hoping that the internet connection would cooperate. Finally the time came, and we saw President Uchtdorf smiling at us on our computer screen.

Called to Serve

After initial greetings, President Uchtdorf said, "You have been called to be a General Authority of the Church and to serve in the First Quorum of the Seventy until age 70. You might come to Salt Lake City for the first year or go somewhere else. Your assignment in an area will begin on August 1. Your service as a full-time General Authority will commence in April, following your sustaining and setting apart."

President Uchtdorf mentioned that I did not need to give any advance notice to my employer, the Church Educational System. "They will find out when you are sustained," he observed. Then he asked, "Do you have any questions?"

We were too stunned to have any questions. When the video conference concluded, Naume and I sat side by side, firmly gripping each other's hands without saying a word. Naume then turned, hugged me, and whispered, "You will be fine! You will make it!" She has always been a great strength to me, and she knew the words I needed to hear at that moment. I responded, "Thank you! Yes, we will make it together!"

The Lord's Errand and the Lord's Help

On Saturday, April 6, 2013, as I took my seat on the stage of the Conference Center with other General Authorities, Naume's reassuring words faded. I felt overwhelmed and inadequate. In my mind, a voice persistently repeated, "You do not belong here! A serious mistake has been made!" The next day, during the Sunday sessions of general conference, my feelings of inadequacy persisted.

I was set apart the following Tuesday morning as a member of the First Quorum of the Seventy. That afternoon, I joined other newly called General Authorities in the upper room of the Salt Lake Temple for a meeting with the seven Presidents of the Seventy. The meeting was directed by the Senior President, Elder Ronald A. Rasband, who is now a member of the Quorum of the Twelve Apostles. As I listened to Elder Rasband talk about his experiences with past and present prophets and apostles, I continued to doubt my ability to serve. Then, as chains of doubt tightened around me, I suddenly heard another voice clearly in my mind: "Edward, it is not about *you*! It is about *me, the Lord*!"

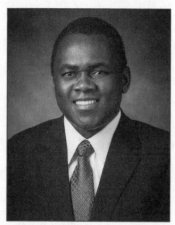

Elder Edward Dube, 2013

Those chains loosened and fell to the ground. I realized that I didn't need to worry about my strengths and weaknesses. I had been called by the Lord. This is His work! All that He required of me was that I keep His commandments, deny myself of all ungodliness, and love Him with all my might, mind, and strength. If I would submit to these requirements, His grace would be sufficient for me! (See Mosiah 2:22; Moroni 10:32.)

Soon after the Lord reminded me of this truth, He allowed me to see it in action in the life of His prophet. Early one morning in the spring of 2013, while I was still receiving my orientation as a newly called General Authority, I saw President Thomas S. Monson walk into the boardroom of the Church Administration Building. He looked very tired as he took his seat. When the meeting began under his direction, I was surprised to see how energetic he was and how engaged he was in the discussion. In my mind's eye, I saw him leave the hospital that morning to come to our meeting. His wife was nearing death, and he had probably slept by her hospital bed the night before. Knowing the urgency of the work ahead of us, he came to the meeting so he could fulfill his responsibilities in the Lord's work. I gained a better understanding of something I had heard him say many times:

"Remember that this work is not yours and mine alone. It is the Lord's work, and when we are on the Lord's errand, we are entitled to the Lord's help. Remember that the Lord will shape the back to bear the burden placed upon it."[34]

Choosing to Trust the Lord

Even after these experiences, I sometimes struggle with feelings of inadequacy and self-doubt. I compare myself to other General Authorities, handicapping my ability to serve. Like Moses, I ask, "Who am I to do this work?" (see Exodus 3:11). President Henry B. Eyring has observed that these thoughts are normal for people like you and me when we are called to do the work of the Lord. "When those feelings of inadequacy strike us," he says, "it is the time to remember the Savior. He assures us that we don't do this work alone."[35]

You and I have a choice to make. We can choose to trust the Lord—to see ourselves as He sees us—or we can choose to live without His guidance and strengthening hand. We can succeed in His work only as we are determined to be His disciples, only as we remember that this work is not about us but about Him, only as we "trust in the Lord with all [our] heart" and "lean not unto [our] own understanding" (Proverbs 3:5). We don't need to compare ourselves against Him or against other people. We just need to trust Him, learn of Him, look to Him, follow Him, and come to Him. And He will help us along the way.

> O ye that embark in the service of God, see that ye serve
> Him with all your heart, might, mind and strength, that
> ye may stand blameless before God at the last day.
> . . . If ye have desires to serve God ye are called to the work.

DOCTRINE AND COVENANTS 4:2–3

CHAPTER 19

Higher Thoughts, Higher Ways

At the end of a powerful sermon, King Benjamin looked out at his people, who were gathered with their families surrounding the temple in Zarahemla. He offered this counsel: "This much I can tell you, that if ye do not watch yourselves, and your thoughts, and your words, and your deeds, and observe the commandments of God, and continue in the faith of what ye have heard concerning the coming of our Lord, even unto the end of your lives, ye must perish. And now, O man, remember, and perish not" (Mosiah 4:30).

King Benjamin had testified of the Savior's ministry and Atonement. He had urged his people to exercise faith, to repent, and to serve God by serving one another. His final exhortation in this sermon focused on thoughts and actions:

- Watch yourselves.
- Watch your thoughts.
- Watch your deeds.
- Observe the commandments of God.

- Continue with faith in Jesus Christ.
- Remember, and perish not.

When I was 21 years old, a friend gave me a similar exhortation.

Think, Think, Think

When I was a young man, I worked for John Newbold, who had a large farm. John occasionally took me with him when he vaccinated his cows. On one such journey, he told me that some of his cows were dying.

"What do you think I can do for the cows?" he asked.

I admitted I didn't have an answer. I hadn't thought about it.

At that point, John pulled his car off the dusty road, stopped, looked straight at me, and said, "Eddie! Think, think, think. If you don't think, you'll die!" Then he shared his own idea to save the cows, and we drove to the farm to carry out his plan.

John's words and example shaped my life. I followed his advice. I started thinking more and translating my thoughts into action. I began pondering what I was doing and what I wanted in life. I worked vigorously to make changes in my environment, knowing that my environment would influence my thoughts. I gave careful attention to the company I kept, the movies I watched, and the books I read. As my thinking changed, I slowly changed from being uninterested and laid-back to being open to the truth and ready to take action. This attitude opened my mind to new, enlightening opportunities—including my first experience reading the Book of Mormon (see chapter 5).

Our Thoughts as They Influence Others

Nine years after that life-changing conversation with John Newbold, I worked for the Church Educational System (CES) in

Harare, Zimbabwe. Along with other CES employees, I was invited to attend a conference in Johannesburg, South Africa. This would be my first experience working with people from other African countries.

CES staff, 1994. Left to right: Raphel Chibota, Upenyu Tambara, Nelson Dibble, Tried Kalipeza, Edward Dube, Clark Dhlomo, and Frank Bradshaw

Africa is a large continent with many different peoples and cultures. For some reason, Naume and I had a misconception about people from Nigeria. Many Nigerians are innovative and confident, and they tend to speak more loudly than other people. We misjudged these characteristics as signs of aggression. Whenever we met Nigerians, we took extra caution. This continued even in meetings with CES personnel. I did not interact with Nigerians at the conference as much as I interacted with others.

Our suspicion toward Nigerians continued for years. We were not plagued by a *lack* of thinking, as I had been as a teenager and young adult. Instead, we were plagued by *prejudiced* thinking.

More than 20 years after that conference in South Africa, I was called to serve as a General Authority. Naume and I did not know much about what my responsibilities would be. We did know, however, that many General Authorities served in Area Presidencies after receiving training in Salt Lake City. We immediately and excitedly assumed that I would be called to serve in our area as a member of the Africa Southeast Area Presidency and that we would live in Johannesburg. We started looking at possible schools for our children in that city.

A week or so later, we received a phone call from Elder Ronald A. Rasband, who was serving at the time as the senior President in the Presidency of the Seventy. He told us that the First Presidency had asked him to inform us of our new assignment. We would move to the Africa West Area, where I would serve as Second Counselor in the Area Presidency. The Africa West Area included Nigeria.

Naume and I were in different places, connected by conference call, when we talked with Elder Rasband. As soon as I got home, I looked at Naume and said, "We love Nigeria and its people, don't we?" Our thinking, perception, and attitude changed—and just in time. When we arrived in Accra, Ghana, Elder LeGrand R. Curtis Jr., the Area President, assigned me to serve the Saints in Nigeria.

Our family spent two rewarding, inspiring years in West Africa, and I spent most of that time serving in Nigeria. Naume often accompanied me, and we grew to love the Nigerian people. We now count many brothers and sisters in Nigeria among our best friends.

We Are What We Think

In my teenage years and some of my young adult years, I was lost in superficial, unfocused thinking. This resulted in a superficial, unfocused life. Years later, I missed out on meaningful friendships with Nigerian brothers and sisters because of my own shallow, prejudiced thinking.

We are what we think.

Elder Dieter F. Uchtdorf observed: "What we love determines what we seek. What we seek determines what we think and do. What we think and do determines who we are—and who we will become."[36] He spoke the truth. We can change our destiny by changing our way of thinking. This takes work, but we can do it.

It may be impossible for shallow thoughts and deep thoughts to demand our attention at the same time. We choose one or the other. The danger is that shallow thinking takes much less effort. We must work vigorously to replace inferior thoughts with quality thoughts. President Spencer W. Kimball quoted an unknown author who said, "The greatest battle of life is fought out within the silent chambers of the soul."[37] For example, Naume and I had to push out, put off, and purge our misperceptions about the people of Nigeria. Then we allowed that space in our minds to be filled with the truth about those good people.

What can we do to influence our own thoughts for good? One thing we can do is control what we feed our minds. I have found that when I begin each day with scripture study and prayer, my life is enriched. I am better prepared to receive guidance from the Lord in my thoughts and decisions. "My thoughts are not your thoughts," the Lord says, "neither are your ways my ways. . . . For as the heavens are higher than the earth, so are my ways higher than your ways, and my thoughts than your thoughts" (Isaiah 55:8–9). In that same revelation, He urges us to seek Him and call upon Him (see Isaiah 55:6). He promises us that His word will be like the rain and snow from heaven that nourishes the earth and brings forth seed. If we allow His thoughts and ways to become ours, we "shall go out with joy, and be led forth with peace" (Isaiah 55:12; see also verses 10–11).

Another thing we can do to improve our thoughts is stop occasionally and think about our thinking—evaluate our efforts to think good thoughts. From time to time, I ask myself the following questions. You might ask yourself the same questions or find other questions that are more helpful for you.

1. What is the quality of my thinking?
2. Am I skilled at analyzing problems?
3. Am I concentrating on the things I need to concentrate on, or am I easily distracted?
4. Am I a deep thinker?
5. How disciplined am I in controlling my thoughts?
6. What steps do I need to take to improve my way of thinking?

Remember Jacob's warning and promise: "To be carnally-minded is death, and to be spiritually-minded is life eternal" (2 Nephi 9:39). Spiritually minded thoughts help us follow the Savior, stay on His covenant path, and see what He sees in us.

As I consider the power of our thoughts to mold our destiny, I am reminded of a dear friend named Betty Sala. Betty was never one to stay in the shade of the mango tree.

When Betty was baptized a member of The Church of Jesus Christ of Latter-day Saints, she lived in a compound near a mine in Arcturus, Zimbabwe. The nearest branch was about 21 kilometers (13 miles) away, and Betty and her family did not have a car. She could have thought, "That's too far. I'll just stay home." Instead, she walked those 21 kilometers each Sunday for Church meetings, often with a child on her back.

Meetings at the branch were conducted in English. Betty

spoke very little English, and she didn't know how to read and write in her native language of Shona. She could have thought, "I can't understand what they are saying. There's no place for me there." But she continued attending church, and her husband, Gibson, often whispered translations to her during meetings. She also enrolled in Gospel Literacy, a course the Church offered to teach people to read and write English. A couple of years after enrolling in this program, she was called as a branch Relief Society president.

Betty and Gibson Sala served diligently in the Church, and they shared the gospel with their family and friends. Eventually, their efforts combined with the efforts of other Latter-day Saints in the area, leading to the creation of the Arcturus Mine Ward. In addition to magnifying their Church callings, they volunteered as seminary and institute teachers. Because of their influence, a number of young men from Arcturus Mine served missions.

I don't know what would have happened if Betty had allowed negative circumstances to lead to negative thoughts, but I know that her positive, faithful thoughts have shaped her destiny—and influenced the destiny of many others.

As he thinketh in his heart, so is he.

PROVERBS 23:7

CHAPTER 20

One Sheep

The Savior taught: "What man of you, having an hundred sheep, if he lose one of them, doth not leave the ninety and nine and go into the wilderness after that which is lost, until he find it? And when he hath found it, he layeth it on his shoulders, rejoicing" (Joseph Smith Translation, Luke 15:4; Luke 15:5).

I have been that one sheep. I have also been that shepherd, striving to follow the example of the Good Shepherd. I have experienced the joy of the rescue from both perspectives.

My Experiences as a Sheep

One Lost Sheep in Kwekwe

After I was baptized and confirmed a member of the Church, I quickly learned that the Kwekwe Branch needed every member—even me. I discovered that whether I prepared and blessed the sacrament, gathered hymnbooks after meetings, arranged chairs, opened windows, greeted investigators, or did any other task, my attendance at church mattered each week. I also learned that weekly attendance was important for me personally. Each

Sunday I gained something new—a principle, an impression, or a simple observation of how others taught and expressed themselves. I eventually connected with the other members of the branch. I felt a sense of belonging.

But when I learned that a festival was coming to my township of Mbizo, Kwekwe, on a Sunday, I faced a conflict. At first, I told my friends that I would join them after Church services. Those friends, who were not members of the Church, knew my weaknesses and the things I liked best. They said, "If you go to church first, you will miss the most fun part of the festival! The barbecue will be finished before you get there." When I woke up on Sunday morning, I chose to go to the barbecue and miss church.

I learned later that morning that the festival had been canceled. It was already too late for me to go to church, so I simply stayed in the one-room apartment I rented. Rather than feeling a sense of belonging, I felt a sense of loss—a big vacuum within me.

At about 12:30 that afternoon, I heard a voice outside the house where I rented a room: "Does Eddie Dube live here?" I wanted to hide under my bed—the only place to hide in my little room. The only other things in the room were a stove, a small cupboard with a few plates and pans, and a clothesline stretched from one side of the bed to the other. A curtain separated my room from the rest of the house. Before I could hide or do anything else, my visitors were standing behind that curtain. They were John and Jean Newbold, my branch president and his wife.

I let them in, knowing exactly why they had come. Sensing my apprehension, they lovingly told me that they missed me at church. We visited for a while, and then they left.

Their words—"Eddie, we missed you. We missed you at

church today!"—kept ringing in my mind that afternoon and throughout the night. I was just one sheep, but I was lost that day. The Lord, in His tender mercy, sent angels to watch over me.

I resolved that I would never deliberately miss church again. And I never have.

One Sheep in Need of Encouragement

A few years later, I was serving a full-time mission in Zimbabwe. I was not a lost sheep, but I was still a sheep who needed tender care. My mission president, Maurice Bateman, must have known that.

Edward with President Maurice Bateman and Sister Analeen Bateman, April 1986

President Bateman felt inspired to give me a leadership assignment. He sent me a letter. "Elder Edward Dube," he said, "I am pleased with your personal example as a missionary, and therefore, you have been assigned to be a district leader in Bulawayo District. Your personal example of diligence in scripture study, effective administration, being sensitive to others' needs, living the mission rules with exactness and carrying out the work of the

mission with all diligence will be a good example for the missionaries in your district."

I read and reread the letter with excitement and apprehension.
I reasoned that my mission president, who was many miles away
in Johannesburg, South Africa, did not know much about me in
faraway Bulawayo, Zimbabwe. I was fairly certain that I was not
the exemplary missionary he described in his letter. But I knew
three things for sure: (1) God knew me, (2) God worked through
His servants, and (3) President Bateman was one of His servants.
I knew that the Lord had said, "My word shall not pass away, but
shall all be fulfilled, whether by my own voice or by the voice of
my servants, it is the same" (Doctrine and Covenants 1:38).

At the end of the letter, President Bateman wrote, "This assignment to serve as a district leader is a sacred trust from the
Lord."

I was humbled by this assignment, and I was determined to
live up to the expectations of my mission president and the Lord.
I went into the living room where the three other missionaries
in the apartment—Elders Lazarus Salizani, Caison F. Jack, and
Raphael Chibota—were chatting with each other. Since the four
of us would form a new district in the mission, I asked if they
would like to read my letter. After they read it, they all excitedly
congratulated me.

I asked for their forgiveness. I said, "I am terribly sorry for
not setting a good example for you. Will you forgive me for not
living up to the mission president's expectations in this letter? I
promise to change and live up to these expectations."

I further asked these great missionaries if they were willing
to help me. They all agreed and expressed their desire to change
as well. I was determined to start following mission rules with

exactness—including the rule to keep our apartment clean. So I walked immediately to the kitchen sink, which was full of dirty dishes, silverware, pots, and pans. I washed all the dirty cookware and mopped the floors. For the next couple of weeks, whenever I saw a knife with peanut butter and jam that had been left in the sink, or a half glass of milk or juice, or wet floors, I would clean up with a big smile. I kept the floors clean and shining and made sure the whole apartment was clean.

I also tried to set an example of diligent service—to go out and share the gospel each day and to return home at the appointed time. I was humbled to see how my fellow servants also started sharing the gospel more diligently. They even washed the dishes and cleaned the apartment! We experienced great success in the work. My companion and I broke a record for the Famona Branch, which was regarded as one of the most difficult areas in the mission for productive missionary work. In a six-month period, we helped 11 people receive the ordinances of baptism and confirmation.

With a simple letter, my mission president had reached out to me—one sheep, 860 kilometers (535 miles) away from him—and had gathered me more securely in the Lord's fold. His leadership and optimism were infectious. His words expanded the vision of all the missionaries in the district. We viewed our adversity in the Famona Branch as a challenging opportunity. Through positive attitude, hard work, obedience, and much fasting and prayer, we qualified for more help from the Lord, and He made us instruments in His hands to bless our brothers and sisters.

We experienced a fulfillment of a promise He gave His servants in the early days of the Church: "You must keep my commandments in all things; and by your hands I will work a marvelous work among the children of men, unto the convincing of many of their sins, that they may come unto repentance, and that they may come unto the kingdom of my Father" (Doctrine and Covenants 18:43–44). We were still His sheep, but we were also shepherds.

My Experiences as a Shepherd

One Lost Sheep Who Wanted to Give Up

Over two decades later, I served as president of the Zimbabwe Harare Mission. Whenever I assigned a missionary to be a district leader, zone leader, or assistant to the president, I sent him a letter outlining his responsibilities and expressing my confidence in him. Those mission leaders served very well. I attribute our success as a mission to their service and to the lessons I learned from my mission president.

In my calling as mission president, I discovered that when missionaries begin their missions, their thoughts wander in different directions. Many new missionaries have limited or no experience working within a tight schedule, getting up early, studying in a disciplined way, planning, setting goals, working with a detailed plan to accomplish goals, and regularly assessing their progress. These requirements are difficult for them at first. As soon as they settle in, really focusing on their missionary purpose, many of their challenges vanish. They slowly gain courage and become prepared to tackle their task. They learn to look up to the Savior, studying the scriptures daily and testifying of His Atonement and the Restoration of His gospel. They conquer homesickness and fears and find joy in service. Their growth over a period of eighteen months to two years is absolutely astounding. Their vision expands, and they become the men and women God knows they can become.

One day I received a phone call about a new missionary who was struggling to make these changes. The president of the Missionary Training Center (MTC) in Johannesburg, South Africa, called and told me that this elder, who was assigned to our mission, wanted to quit and return home. The MTC president had spoken with the missionary's stake president, who had said that the missionary should come home if that was what he wanted to do.

I asked the MTC president to send the missionary to our mission. If he really needed to return home, he could leave from there. I reasoned that he had already flown more than 20 hours from his home in the United States of America, and a 90-minute flight to Zimbabwe was nothing by comparison. Going to Zimbabwe would enhance his experience.

The missionary agreed and came. When he arrived with the other missionaries, I interviewed him. He told me the same thing he had told the MTC president. "I am not happy here," he said. "I really want to go home." He wanted to serve—he had always wanted to serve a mission—but he was terribly homesick. I asked him to do his best for three weeks, which would give him time to enjoy the association with his companion and the friendly people he would meet in his assigned area.

At the end of those three weeks, the missionary was back in my office with the same plea: "I want to go home." Praying for help in that moment, I did my best to strengthen and support him. I ministered to him individually, as though he was the only missionary I had, even though 159 other missionaries were spread among the countries of Malawi, Zambia, and Zimbabwe. I thought of the Savior's counsel: "If a man have an hundred sheep, and one of them be gone astray, doth he not leave the ninety and nine, and goeth into the mountains, and seeketh that which is gone astray?" (Matthew 18:12).

Over the next six months, this missionary occasionally had dinner with me. As we talked during one of our meetings, he told me that his sister had sent him a letter, sharing the sad news that their mother was recovering in the hospital after a suicide attempt. The sister assured him that if he would show her letter to me, I would certainly allow him to return home. When he shared the letter with me, we both shed tears. I then asked him if he wanted to stay on his mission or go home. He responded that he was confused and did not know what to do, so we spent some time reading the scriptures together. As we continued talking, I asked him what he enjoyed at home. He said that he liked to play golf, so we scheduled a time for him to teach me how to play.

This elder stayed on his mission and continued meeting with me. Each time we met, he would get a burst of energy and would serve with renewed dedication. But then the homesickness would return.

Although this young man and I developed a bond of friendship, I eventually became discouraged about his situation. I was ready to give up and send him home. Then one night he and many other missionaries were at the mission home. We had just watched the Saturday afternoon session of the October 2010 general conference, and we were waiting for the priesthood session. Since we were watching the sessions live, it was past midnight in Harare. Some of us were outside, and this young man came and stood next to me. He simply said, "President, I have decided to stay."

I could hardly believe what he had said. I asked him, "Why have you decided to stay and serve your mission?"

He said that he felt it was the right thing to do. Then he added, "I decided to stay not for myself, but for my children and grandchildren."

We embraced and rejoiced together. I felt the truth of the Savior's words about the shepherd who finds one lost sheep: "And if so be that he find it, verily I say unto you, he rejoiceth more of that sheep, than of the ninety and nine which went not astray" (Matthew 18:13).

This young man became one of our strongest missionaries. He inspired other missionaries to look up to the Lord and serve with humility, faith, and power. Toward the end of his two years in Africa, he asked to extend his mission so that he could make up for the six months he had lost. The Missionary Department approved a twelve-week extension for him.

Now he and his sweetheart have been sealed in the temple, and they are noble, righteous parents. His decision to stay on his mission surely has brought blessings to his family, and it will continue to do so forever.

One Lost Sheep with a Gun

In February 2016, I went to the southern United States to preside at a stake conference. Responding to an assignment from President Russell M. Nelson, who was then serving as President of the Quorum of the Twelve Apostles, I had reached out to the stake president in advance, asking him to work with bishops to identify families and individuals who could benefit from us visiting them.

All the members we visited were facing serious challenges: crises of faith, illness, apathy about the Church, pain because of bad choices of their loved ones. All of them but one welcomed us graciously in their homes.

That one unwelcoming sheep never let us in his house. He approached us just after we got out of the car. Shabbily dressed and with anger in his eyes, he growled, "What do you want?" The stake president explained who we were and that we had been sent by his bishop. In response, this man pulled a pistol from his jacket and waved it at us. He said that he had had terrible experiences in the past and that he did not trust anyone.

I am very afraid of guns. At that moment I wanted to grab the stake president and pull him to the car, but the stake president was not intimidated by this brother or his gun. Rather than running away, he showed love and compassion and continued with the conversation.

Realizing that the stake president was not going to leave, I tried to change the subject. I struggled for something to say but finally managed to stammer, "I love those cows. I saw them behind your house. Would you mind if we go and look at them?"

The brother responded by waving his gun at me and warning, "Don't try anything funny!" Then he walked toward the back of the house, and I followed him. As I walked, I heard the still, small voice of the Spirit prompting me to speak. And so I turned and walked closer to the man, looked in his eyes, and said, "President Monson loves you. Would you accept the love for you from the Lord's prophet?"

He paused for a moment, looked down, looked up at me, and started weeping. He told us what he was going through. His wife, who was not a member of the Church, was suffering from depression. He had just lost his job. He was trying to get an education and support his wife and two little children.

We had a good conversation, and I asked if we could share his problems with the bishop, who would know how to help him and his family. He said we could. I was thankful that the Holy Ghost had prompted me to mention President Thomas S. Monson, who at the time was the only person authorized to exercise all priesthood keys on the earth. President Monson had asked us to express his love for all the members of the Church—a pattern followed by all Presidents of the Church, including President Monson's successor, President Russell M. Nelson. In this case, an expression of the prophet's love for one person was just what was needed to soften that person's heart.

A few weeks later, I followed up with the stake president regarding this brother and his family. The stake president reported that the man who once waved a gun at us was now welcoming the bishop, the ward council, and the full-time missionaries into his home to help him and his family.

This experience taught me a great lesson. I had been intimidated by the man's shabby dress, angry eyes, harsh voice, and gun. At first, I had failed to see him as the Lord saw him. I am thankful for the persistence and compassion of the stake president, who exercised his priesthood keys to search the heart of a brother and sense his need. This dedicated priesthood leader was true to the Lord's words to the prophet Samuel: "Look not on his countenance, . . . for the Lord seeth not as man seeth; for man looketh on the outward appearance, but the Lord looketh on the heart" (1 Samuel 16:7). The stake president saw beyond the things that intimidated me. He looked at this man as a brother and caught a glimpse of what God saw in Him.

Sometimes this is all we need to help a sheep return to the fold.

Remember the worth of souls is great in the sight of God. . . .

And if it so be that you should labor all your days
in crying repentance unto this people, and bring,
save it be one soul unto me, how great shall be
your joy with him in the kingdom of my Father!

And now, if your joy will be great with one soul
that you have brought unto me in the kingdom
of my Father, how great will be your joy if
you should bring many souls unto me!

DOCTRINE AND COVENANTS 18:10, 15–16

CHAPTER 21

An Eye Single to the Glory of God

The Lord has said that "faith, hope, charity and love, with an eye single to the glory of God, qualify [us] for [His] work" (Doctrine and Covenants 4:5).

What does it mean to have "an eye single to the glory of God"? Sister Patricia T. Holland—who serves and teaches with power and compassion next to her husband, Elder Jeffrey R. Holland— taught that to have an eye single to God's glory is to stop "performing for the admiration of mortals" and to seek "honestly and faithfully to glorify only God." She said, "I promise you that if . . . your eye is fixed, centered, riveted, and so cemented that it cannot be distracted by the allure of the crowds or the vanities of this world—then you will hear your calling from God."[38]

Hearing Our Calling from God

When I think of hearing our calling from God, I think of the prophet Nephi, son of Sariah and Lehi. We often quote Nephi's powerful words: "I will go and do the things which the Lord hath commanded, for I know that the Lord giveth no commandments unto the children of men, save he shall prepare a way for them that they may accomplish the thing which he commandeth them" (1 Nephi 3:7).

Sometimes we might forget Nephi's personal preparation to be able to make such a bold statement, and sometimes we might not think enough about the surprising things the Lord required him to do once he made that commitment.

Before Nephi had the faith and strength to "go and do," his parents guided him to learn the ways of the Lord. "Having been born of goodly parents," he said, "therefore I was taught" (1 Nephi 1:1). And Nephi did more than simply listen to his parents' teachings. Unlike his older brothers Laman and Lemuel, he sought to know for himself at a young age. He said: "Having great desires to know of the mysteries of God, wherefore, I did cry unto the Lord; and behold he did visit me, and did soften my heart that I did believe all the words which had been spoken by my father; wherefore, I did not rebel against him like unto my brothers" (1 Nephi 2:16).

Nephi's humility is a great lesson to me. He wanted to understand the mysteries of God that his father had taught him, so he prayed and allowed the Lord to soften his heart. He followed the pattern the Lord would teach centuries later to Moroni: "If men come unto me I will show unto them their weakness. I give unto men weakness that they may be humble; and my grace is sufficient for all men that humble themselves before me; for if they humble themselves before me, and have faith in me, then will I make weak things become strong unto them" (Ether 12:27).

To Nephi, the Lord said: "Blessed art thou . . . because of thy faith, for thou hast sought me diligently, with lowliness of heart. And inasmuch as ye shall keep my commandments, ye shall prosper, and shall be led to a land of promise" (1 Nephi 2:19–20). With this promise came a surprising and challenging calling: "Thou shalt be made a ruler and a teacher over thy brethren" (1 Nephi 2:22).

Directly after receiving these words from the Lord, Nephi received an assignment. His father told him that he and his brothers were to go to Jerusalem and the house of the politically powerful Laban. They were to obtain from Laban a set of brass plates, which contained a record of the Jews and a genealogy of their family. This was when Nephi uttered those now-famous words, declaring that he would "go and do."

It is interesting to note that when Nephi and his brothers came near Jerusalem, Nephi did not seem to have the same energetic faith he had expressed to his father. Rather than seeking the Lord's guidance on what to do, he consulted with his brothers, and they cast lots to determine which of them would approach Laban and ask for the plates. I wonder if perhaps Nephi secretly hoped the lot wouldn't fall on him. Maybe he was relieved when the "lot fell upon Laman; and Laman went in unto the house of Laban" (1 Nephi 3:11). Laban angrily thrust Laman out of his presence and threatened to kill him, and Laman narrowly escaped out of the city.

That was enough for Nephi's brothers. They had tried to get the brass plates and had failed. They were upset with Nephi, and they were ready to go back empty-handed to their family in the wilderness (see 1 Nephi 3:12–14). But Nephi swore an oath: "As the Lord liveth, and as we live, we will not go down unto our father in the wilderness until we have accomplished the thing which the Lord hath commanded us" (1 Nephi 3:15).

Speaking of Nephi's bold statement, Elder Bruce R.

McConkie taught: "Nephi made God his partner. If he failed to get the plates, it meant God had failed. And because God does not fail, it was incumbent upon Nephi to get the plates or lay down his life in the attempt."[39]

This story is familiar to Latter-day Saints throughout the world. Nephi and his brothers decided to try again. This time, they gathered the gold, silver, and precious things they had left in their home and attempted to trade them for the brass plates. Laban thrust them all out, sent his servants to kill them, and stole their treasures.

After another narrow escape from Laban, the brothers once again found themselves outside the city of Jerusalem. Now Laman and Lemuel were even more upset with Nephi, even after an angel came and commanded them to go to Jerusalem again. They were ready to abandon their mission (1 Nephi 3:16–31). Any ordinary person would feel the same. But Nephi said, "Let us go up again unto Jerusalem, and let us be faithful in keeping the commandments of the Lord; for behold he is mightier than all the earth, then why not mightier than Laban and his fifty, yea, or even than his tens of thousands?" (1 Nephi 4:1).

Nephi's brothers continued to be angry with him, but they went to the walls of the city anyway. They hid there while he went inside alone. With an eye single to the glory of God, Nephi "was led by the Spirit, not knowing beforehand the things which [he] should do" (1 Nephi 4:6). And with an eye single to the glory of God, he obtained the brass plates in a way he never would have planned. (See 1 Nephi 4:4–38.)

Examining the story of Nephi and his brothers, we see that callings from the Lord—whether they are official Church callings or personal promptings to serve—require our courage and energy.

We also see that when we give of ourselves to serve others, the Lord blesses us with increased courage and energy. On the other hand, we lose courage and energy when we hold back or choose not to serve. We must keep our eye single to the glory of God, even when difficulties arise and even when we are surprised by the tasks the Lord requires of us.

Moving Forward with Surprises and Opportunities to Serve

Like Nephi, we might sometimes receive what Elder Neal A. Maxwell called "a customized commandment"[40]—something the Lord requires only of us. Sometimes those customized commandments might take us by surprise. Sometimes we might need to be "chastened and tried, even as Abraham" (Doctrine and Covenants 101:4). These commands always give us opportunities to serve.

I received one of those surprises when I was serving in the Area Presidency of the Africa West Area. Elder LeGrand R. Curtis Jr. was Area President, Elder Terrence M. Vinson was First Counselor, and I was Second Counselor. In early 2015, we

Africa West Area Presidency, 2013–2015. Left to right: Elder Terence M. Vinson, Elder LeGrand Curtis Jr., and Elder Edward Dube

ordered personalized letterhead and envelopes for our official correspondence. We assumed that Elder Curtis and Elder Vinson would receive assignments to leave the area before I would, so I purchased over a thousand sheets of letterhead that included my name and my assignment in the Africa West Area. A few months later, I received an assignment to serve in Salt Lake City.

What could I do with all that stationery? I didn't want to waste it. Was there a purpose in the huge pile of paper and envelopes in my office?

With help from my assistant, Dinah De-Graft Mensah, I came up with a plan. Sister Mensah and I asked each stake president and mission president in Nigeria to send us a list of 25 less-active members in their stake or district. We requested that they consider members who were most likely to respond to an invitation to return to full activity in the Church.

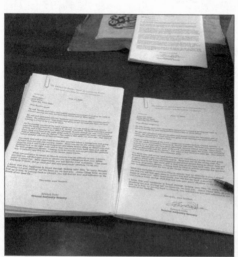

Letters Elder Dube sent to Saints in Nigeria

I wrote a letter of testimony and invitation, and we printed more than a thousand copies on my letterhead. As I signed each letter personally, I thought of the Savior Jesus Christ when He came to minister to the surviving people of the Nephites. Immediately after, He testified of His mission as the Son of God and "the light and life of the world" (3 Nephi 11:11). He invited them to come forth and thrust their hands into His side and feel the prints of the nails in His hands and feet. "And this they did do, going forth one by one until they had all gone forth" (3 Nephi 11:15; see also verse 14). In my small way, I was reaching out to people one at a time and inviting them to come, one by one, back to their Savior.

Some of those members sent letters back to me. Their comments of gratitude were truly humbling. I do not know what happened to others, but I know how I felt when I signed each letter. I felt that my transfer from the Africa West Area and my specific assignment in Nigeria did not signal the end of my ministry among those Saints I loved so much.

We do our best to plan our lives, remembering these words from the Lord: "My thoughts are not your thoughts, neither are your ways my ways" (Isaiah 55:8). We also remember these comforting and inspiring words:

"Draw near unto me and I will draw near unto you; seek me diligently and ye shall find me; ask, and ye shall receive; knock, and it shall be opened unto you. . . .

"And if your eye be single to my glory, your whole bodies shall be filled with light, and there shall be no darkness in you; and that body which is filled with light comprehendeth all things.

"Therefore, sanctify yourselves that your minds become single to God, and the days will come that you shall see him; for he will unveil his face unto you, and it shall be in his own time, and in his own way, and according to his own will" (Doctrine and Covenants 88:63, 67–68).

Sometimes He unveils His face to us in surprisingly simple ways—like when he gave me a stack of seemingly useless stationery and inspired me to use it to bless His children. And what a joy it is for us to serve as instruments in His hands!

> And if it so be that the children of men keep the commandments of God he doth nourish them, and strengthen them, and provide means whereby they can accomplish the thing which he has commanded them.
>
> 1 NEPHI 17:3

Easy Yoke and Light Burden

In December 2017 in Madziva, Zimbabwe, Naume and I saw a man plowing his field with a team of two oxen. I was amazed to see that one animal was a huge ox and the other was a small bullock. I was perplexed. I wondered aloud, "Why would a farmer plow with two unequal animals in the yoke?"

Naume's mother, who was standing nearby, pointed to the yoke. I looked more closely and saw traces connecting the yoke to the bullock. The large ox was pulling all the weight, and the tiny bullock was being broken in, learning how to plow.

I immediately thought of the Lord's invitation: "Come unto me, all ye that labour and are heavy laden, and I will give you rest. Take my yoke upon you, and learn of me; for I am meek and lowly in heart: and ye shall find rest unto your souls" (Matthew 11:28–29). In a normal yoking, the load is distributed equally. When we are yoked with Jesus Christ, He bears the heaviness of the load. Our load is not so heavy, but He allows us to share in the joy of the labor.

To properly understand the Lord's gracious offer to allow us to take His yoke upon ourselves, we need to understand its context. Just before He extended the invitation, He upbraided cities where people had not repented even though they had seen His mighty works (see Matthew 11:20–24). It was to those people that He offered the relief, joy, and grace of His yoke. Today, He continues to extend this invitation to all—to the corrupt, the curious, and the converted. Anyone can choose a deeper level of commitment, take His yoke upon himself or herself, and learn of Him.

Let's take a closer look at the Savior's invitation in Matthew 11:28–30.

"Come unto Me"

With the words "come unto me," Jesus Christ expresses His desire to relieve us from pain, sadness, and oppression. This appeal shows His compassionate heart. It also presents a challenge, because with the words "come unto me," He commands us to turn away from whatever we presently give our attention and dependence. It is a call to turn our lives over to Him completely. The Savior invites us to come directly to Him—not to a program, a system, or an organization. And He sends this plea to all people throughout the world—not to any one group, class, or nationality.

I reflected on this invitation as a new member of The Church of Jesus Christ of Latter-day Saints. I made a conscious decision to follow the Savior in every way possible and to strive to develop His attributes. I committed to give my all. This required that I let go of some ancestral traditions and beliefs. For example, all my life I had been taught that my deceased ancestors were protectors and intermediaries between God and me. I knew that I needed to leave that tradition behind and exercise faith in Christ, who said, "I am the way, the truth, and the life: no man cometh unto the

Father, but by me" (John 14:6). I needed to trust Him. I needed to come unto Him.

"Take My Yoke upon You"

The Savior's invitation to take His yoke upon ourselves is a call to discipleship, a call to serve. He says, "Inasmuch as ye have done it unto one of the least of these my brethren, ye have done it unto me" (Matthew 25:40). The Lord continually calls us to serve others.

I have found that I serve best when I work within the strength He gives me. He is always there beside me if I will yield my life to Him. The load of service becomes overly burdensome only when I try to take over and handle it myself. I feel unable to fulfill a call to serve only when I neglect to trust in the Lord's wisdom, strength, gentleness, and goodness—when I look at the yoke He offers and think it does not fit me. But I feel hope when I remember that He has designed the yoke perfectly for me, a unique individual with a unique combination of gifts, abilities, and weaknesses. He has designed it to help me become more like Him—and He joins me in that yoke! I am like the young bullock I saw in Madziva, plowing next to a yokefellow who is carrying the burden.

"Learn of Me"

In addition to inviting us to come to Him and accept His yoke, the Savior invites us to learn of Him. We learn of Him as we serve—as we accept His call to lift and strengthen others and invite them to come unto Him as well.

We also learn of Him as we study His word. He once spoke to a group of people who sought to kill Him because He said He was the Son of God. He encouraged them to "search the scriptures."

They thought that in those sacred texts they had eternal life. But He said the scriptures "are they which testify of me" (John 5:39). The scriptures have power because they testify of Him. We learn of Him as we study, and He provides the way for us to receive eternal life.

"Ye Shall Find Rest unto Your Souls"

The Savior promises that when we come unto Him, take His yoke upon ourselves, and learn of Him, we "shall find rest unto [our] souls" (Matthew 11:29). This does not mean that He will always remove the challenges and difficulties we face. Instead, He will "ease the burdens which are put upon [our] shoulders, that even [we] cannot feel them upon [our] backs" (Mosiah 24:14). As we exercise faith in Him, follow Him, and "submit cheerfully and with patience" to His will (Mosiah 24:15), regardless of the trials we face, His promise is real: "Lift up your heads and be of good comfort, for I know of the covenant which ye have made unto me; and I will covenant with my people and deliver them out of bondage" (Mosiah 24:13).

President Dallin H. Oaks testified, "The healing power of the Lord Jesus Christ—whether it removes our burdens or strengthens us to endure and live with them like the Apostle Paul—is available for every affliction in mortality."[41]

With open, outstretched arms, Christ invites us to come unto Him and receive healing and strength, "that [we] may be lifted up at the last day and enter into his rest" (Alma 13:29).

A Continual Process

For me, coming unto Christ is a continual process. The Savior has blessed me in my imperfect efforts to accept His invitation. He has helped me begin to move beyond the shade of the mango tree—beyond the boy I once was, beyond the man I thought I would become, and even beyond the limits of this earthly existence. He has helped me begin to partake of the fruit of another tree: the tree of life.

I hope we will all remember and embrace the Savior's invitation. As we strive to come unto Him, learn of Him, and take His yoke upon ourselves, we begin to see Him as He really is. And He begins to teach us who we really are: God's divine children with a divine destiny.

> Cast about your eyes and begin to believe in the Son of God, that he will come to redeem his people. . . .
>
> Plant this word in your hearts, and as it beginneth to swell even so nourish it by your faith. And behold, it will become a tree, springing up in you unto everlasting life. And then may God grant unto you that your burdens may be light, through the joy of his Son. And even all this can ye do if ye will.
>
> ALMA 33:22–23

Notes

1. David O. McKay, *Gospel Ideals: Selections from the Discourses of David O. McKay* (1953), 452.
2. Jeffrey R. Holland, "The Ministry of Angels," *Ensign* or *Liahona*, Nov. 2008.
3. First Presidency letter, February 11, 1999, in *Liahona*, Dec. 1999; see also J. Reuben Clark Jr., meeting of general Church auxiliary executives, March 29, 1940, quoted in Thomas S. Monson, "Bring Him Home," *Ensign* or *Liahona*, Nov. 2003; First Presidency letter, 1962, quoted in Thomas S. Monson, "Heavenly Homes, Forever Families," *Ensign,* Oct. 1991.
4. Henry B. Eyring, "Inquire of the Lord" (remarks at an evening with Elder Neal A. Maxwell, Feb. 2, 2001), 1.
5. Russell M. Nelson, "Set in Order Thy House," *Ensign* or *Liahona*, Nov. 2001.
6. C. S. Lewis, *Mere Christianity,* rev. ed. (1960), 126.
7. Dieter F. Uchtdorf, "Come, Join with Us," *Ensign* or *Liahona*, Nov. 2013; see also F. F. Bosworth, *Christ the Healer* (1924), 23.
8. "I Am a Child of God," *Hymns*, no. 301.
9. Dallin H. Oaks, "Powerful Ideas," *Ensign,* Nov. 1995.
10. Tad R. Callister, *The Blueprint of Christ's Church* (2015), 242–43.

11. Callister, *Blueprint of Christ's Church*, 244.

12. David A. Bednar, "Clean Hands and a Pure Heart," *Ensign* or *Liahona,* Nov. 2007.

13. "I Stand All Amazed," *Hymns,* no. 193.

14. See chapter 2 in this book.

15. D. Todd Christofferson, "When Thou Art Converted," *Ensign* or *Liahona,* May 2004.

16. Boyd K. Packer, "The Candle of the Lord," *Ensign,* Jan. 1983.

17. Dieter F. Uchtdorf, "Missionary Work: Sharing What Is in Your Heart," *Ensign* or *Liahona*, May 2019.

18. Henry B. Eyring, "Mountains to Climb," *Ensign* or *Liahona,* May 2012.

19. Ezra Taft Benson, "To the Single Adult Brethren of the Church," *Ensign*, May 1988.

20. Benson, "To the Single Adult Brethren of the Church."

21. "The Family: A Proclamation to the World," *Ensign* or *Liahona*, Nov. 2010.

22. Thomas S. Monson, "Consider the Blessings," *Ensign* or *Liahona*, Nov. 2012.

23. Dieter F. Uchtdorf, "Faith of Our Father," *Ensign* or *Liahona*, May 2008.

24. Dallin H. Oaks, "The Gospel Culture," *Ensign,* Mar. 2012.

25. "Appendix 1: First Theological Lecture on Faith, circa January–May 1835," 1, Joseph Smith Papers, josephsmithpapers.org/paper -summary/appendix-1-first-theological-lecture-on-faith-circa -january-may-1835/1#facts.

26. See "Secretary-General's Statement on Zimbabwe," July 22, 2005, United Nations, https://www.un.org/sg/en/content/sg/statement /2005-07-22/secretary-generals-statement-zimbabwe.

27. Thomas S. Monson, June 2004 Worldwide Leadership Training Broadcast, ChurchofJesusChrist.org.

28. Russell M. Nelson, "Jesus Christ—the Master Healer," *Ensign* or *Liahona*, Nov. 2005.

29. David A. Bednar, "The Windows of Heaven," *Ensign* or *Liahona*, Nov. 2013.

30. Russell M. Nelson, "Thou Shalt Have No Other Gods," *Ensign*, May 1996.

31. Russell M. Nelson, *Teachings of Russell M. Nelson* (2018), 182–83.

32. *Preach My Gospel* (2019), 1.

33. Russell M. Nelson, "Thou Shalt Have No Other Gods," *Ensign*, May 1996.

34. Thomas S. Monson, "To Learn, to Do, to Be," *Ensign* or *Liahona,* Nov. 2008.

35. Henry B. Eyring, "O Ye That Embark," *Ensign* or *Liahona,* Nov. 2008.

36. Dieter F. Uchtdorf, "The Love of God," *Ensign* or *Liahona,* Nov. 2009.

37. In Spencer W. Kimball, *The Miracle of Forgiveness* (1969), 235; see also Brigham Clegg, "Speakers' Contest: 'Sacrifice,'" *Improvement Era* 5, no. 9 (July 1902): 684.

38. Patricia T. Holland, "An Eye Single," 2, 3, https://speeches.byu.edu /wp-content/uploads/pdf/Holland_Patricia_1985_09.pdf.

39. Bruce R. McConkie, "The Doctrine of the Priesthood," *Ensign*, Apr. 1982.

40. Neal A. Maxwell, "The Pathway of Discipleship," *Ensign*, Sept. 1998.

41. Dallin H. Oaks, "He Heals the Heavy Laden," *Ensign* or *Liahona,* Nov. 2006.